CULTURE SHOCK!
Taiwan

Chris and Ling-li Bates

AR...
5000 S. SAN...
P.O. BOX 90...
LITTLETON, CO 80160-9002

Graphic Arts Center Publishing Company
Portland, Oregon

In the same series

Australia	*Israel*	*South Africa*	*A Globe-Trotter's Guide*
Borneo	*Italy*	*Spain*	*A Student's Guide*
Britain	*Japan*	*Sri Lanka*	*A Traveller's Medical Guide*
Burma	*Korea*	*Switzerland*	*A Wife's Guide*
Canada	*Malaysia*	*Syria*	
China	*Morocco*	*Thailand*	
France	*Nepal*	*USA*	
Hong Kong	*Norway*	*USA—The South*	
India	*Pakistan*	*Vietnam*	
Indonesia	*Philippines*		
Ireland	*Singapore*		

Illustrations by TRIGG
Photographs from Christopher Bates

© 1995 Times Editions Pte Ltd
Reprinted 1995, 1996

This book is published by special
arrangement with Times Editions Pte Ltd
Times Centre, 1 New Industrial Road, Singapore 536196
International Standard Book Number 1-55868-175-2
Library of Congress Catalog Number 94-076068
Graphic Arts Center Publishing Company
P.O. Box 10306 • Portland, Oregon 97210 • (503) 226-2402

All rights reserved. No part of this publication
may be reproduced, stored in a retrieval system,
or transmitted, in any form or by any means,
electronic, mechanical, photocopying, recording
or otherwise, without the prior permission of
the copyright owner.

Printed in Singapore

*We dedicate this book to
Diana, Ethan and Richard—
the best of both worlds.*

SEP 2 3 2003

CONTENTS

Acknowledgements *6*
Introduction *7*

1 The History of the First 'Little Tiger' *11*
2 Touchdown Taiwan *25*
3 Settling In *34*
4 Language *70*
5 The Weight of Tradition *94*
6 Relating to Your Taiwanese Friends *118*
7 Cuisine of the Ilha Formosa *157*
8 Enjoying Taiwan *180*
9 Shengyi—The Meaning of Life *203*
10 Staying Healthy and Handling Emergencies *227*

Cultural Quiz *243*
Bibliography *250*
The Authors *253*
Index *254*

ACKNOWLEDGEMENTS

Many thanks to our friends who discussed their experiences and shared their perceptions of Taiwan with us, especially Dini and Mark. Kudos to Robyn and Diane for their insights on cross-cultural relations, Confucianism, and the spirit of independence.

INTRODUCTION

You have chosen a fascinating country to visit, a country filled with splendor, richness, pristine vistas, solitude, tradition...as well as all their opposites! Taiwan is a place of contradictions begging to be explored, enjoyed, and contemplated. Few locations of such a small size can boast snow-peaked alpine mountains, bountiful plains, and tropical beaches, all within a few hours' drive of each other. And culturally it is just as diverse. On the one hand you can find yourself surrounded by the ancient traditions of the Chinese, as you visit temples and festivals, or watch the *tai chi* practitioners commune with the *Tao* in the park; on the other, you can be caught up in the bustle of Taiwan's state-of-the-art department stores and trendy boutiques, selling an international diversity of goods and designer products.

Taiwan is the home of a Chinese-speaking population of hard-working, hard-playing people. The more you know about them and their country, the more you will enjoy your stay and the less will be your culture shock. In trying to introduce Taiwan and the Taiwanese to you, we have placed major emphasis on the subject of communication, which is usually a major source of frustration to any foreigner. This does not simply involve trying to cope with communicating in a foreign language. One must always remember that Taiwan is a 'high context' culture, in other words a culture in which much is communicated beyond the words that are spoken. Tone of voice, facial expression, physical proximity, body contact, hand action, eye action, and ritual all become part of the dialogue. A fundamental stumbling block in cross-cultural communications occurs when people from a low context culture and those from a high context culture try to communicate, or when the unstated meanings of visual cues and body language differ significantly between parties in the communication.

In Taiwan, people will be reading as much into *how* you communicate as w*hat* you are actually saying. Much of this book is devoted to helping you understand what you are communicating, what they are communicating, and how the messages can be made clear.

Major emphasis is also placed on things that are important to the Taiwanese and why. It is our experience that a major component of culture shock is the 'alienness' of the culture one enters. This may sound facile, but many guides to Taiwan might tell you some point about the country without delving into the why and wherefore. For example, a guidebook might state that "the concept of 'face' is important to Chinese" and yet not explain why and what you should do about it. We hope that by reading this book such questions will be sufficiently dealt with so that you can develop coping strategies. A tactic frequently used in the following chapters is to walk you through environments and situations you may well experience during your stay. Reading through such experiences should make them less alien or shocking to you when the time comes for you yourself to dive in and encounter similar situations.

There are several ways to use *Culture Shock! Taiwan*. If you have the time, read it once all the way through. It will give you a clear idea of the historic foundation and traditions that underlie the cultural phenomena you will see about you. It will give you insights into how your Taiwanese counterparts think. It is also full of practical tips on getting settled in. Alternatively, if you are already on your way or have arrived in a bewildered funk, you may want to use the chapter headings or index to turn to information of immediate concern. Once you have been in Taiwan for a settling-in period, you may want to re-read some relevant chapters, such as 'Relating to Your Taiwanese Friends' or 'The Weight of Tradition'. You can then reflect on how your experiences and what you have seen have been influenced by their culture.

This book distills our experience garnered during 16 years of contact with Taiwan as an American and 16 years of contact with

Westerners as a Taiwanese. We have, therefore, often moved at the interface of the Taiwan/Western community. Where we felt our experience was uncharacteristic, we have discussed the issue with other Westerners and Taiwanese to achieve a broader perspective. Much of the information about arrivals and settling in pertains to Taipei. This seems to be the jumping-off point for most residents as well as short-term explorers of the island.

Lastly, a note about romanizations. As you will learn in more detail in the Chapter Four, there are many ways of writing Chinese using a Western alphabet. In this book, we are using the Yale system because we feel it most closely matches the sounds needed to be spoken and may help you learn to pronounce the terms more authentically. When romanizing Taiwanese place names or Chinese terms widely known in the West, we employ the spelling method common in Taiwan plus the Yale version in italics and parentheses so you will know how to say it. Taipei, for instance, is romanized (and pronounced) *Taibei* in the Yale system. Terms and phrases not commonly known in the West will be romanized directly in the Yale system, with the translation in parentheses. For example, *Ni hau ma?* (How are you?).

We hope you will enjoy your stay in Taiwan and that this book can increase your pleasure, decrease anxiety and misunderstanding, and make your visit a growing experience. Happy trails to you!

Chris and Ling-li Bates

Taiwan is a land of contrasts: some beautiful and dramatic countryside belies the industrial images usually associated with this economically prosperous island.

Chapter One

THE HISTORY OF THE FIRST 'LITTLE TIGER'

It may seem odd to begin a discussion of the history of Taiwan with a description of its geography, but in Taiwan's case its geography created its history. Set as it is betwixt so many cultures, a green jewel in a blue sea, Taiwan was an island fated to serve as a pawn in the geopolitical games of nations, on several occasions becoming a diplomatic 'hot potato'. The modern economic miracle that we see before us today cannot be divorced from this fact. Taiwan's geopolitical status at various stages throughout history lay the foundations for

11

its extraordinary evolution into the first of the 'Little Asian Tiger' economies, later to be joined by Singapore, South Korea and Hong Kong.

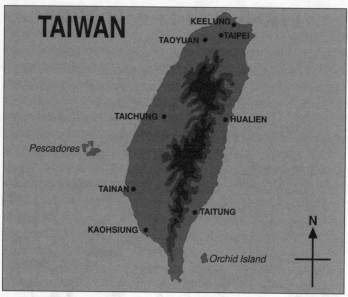

Taiwan is a leaf-shaped island running north to south, approximately 280 miles long by 60 miles wide. It is sandwiched between the South China Sea and the Pacific Ocean. One hundred miles to its west is the Chinese province of Fujian (*Fukkien*). To the northeast lies the Ryukyu chain of islands that comprise present-day Okinawa, while beyond these, roughly 1,200 miles away, is mainland Japan. On Taiwan's southernmost horizon is the first northern island of the Philippine chain.

Taiwan belongs to the Pacific's 'Rim of Fire'. It is volcanic in origin and experiences frequent earthquakes. A ridge of glorious mountains runs north-south down the center of the island. This range has over 100 peaks and exceeds 9,900 feet in height. Bisecting the island east-west is the Tropic of Cancer. The eastern face of Taiwan rises precipitously from the blue Pacific, while the lush western plains drop gradually into the silty China Sea. The island lies right in the corridor most frequented by typhoons (a word that comes from the Mandarin *taifeng*) and the east coast is regularly battered by these winds during the typhoon season. In Taipei, it is true that, apart from several hot and humid months in the summer, the weather is generally miserable, resulting in the popular saying, "Taipei weather is like a stepmother's temper."

Early settlers

The first settlers in Taiwan migrated from Luzon and Malaysia. There were eight distinct language groups, so it is obvious that settlement came in waves and from different places. These settlers populated the coastal regions and engaged in hunting and rudimentary farming. They also engaged in intertribal warfare and head-hunting. They were primitive peoples without a written language, but with a tradition of storytelling and ritual. Today, about a quarter million of these original settlers remain in Taiwan, where their interests have been protected since 1945 by the Nationalist government.

The Chinese

The first political power to take notice of Taiwan was China. For centuries China has been called *Junggwo*, the 'Middle Kingdom'. It placed itself at the center of all nations. Emperors expected tribute from bordering nations, payment of which they felt constituted the subservience of these nations. Tibet, Burma, Thailand, Vietnam, Japan, Korea and Mongolia all paid tribute from time to time. Nations that refused were sometimes attacked, though another ploy was to try to marry a Chinese princess to the ruler to bring them in line. China felt it was the focal point of the political and cultural universe. Thousands of years of political sophistication, urban merchantry, exquisite crafts, and high art all added to this image the Chinese possessed of themselves. Even being taken over by Mongols and Manchus at different periods in time did not decrease this sense of superiority. The Chinese acculturated the new emperors and harmony returned.

But when we speak of 'Chinese', what is actually meant? Modern China lays claim to many ethnic minorities, including Tibetans. But it is the Han Chinese, originating in the valleys and flood plains of the Yangtze (*Chang Jiang*) and Yellow (*Hwang He*) rivers, who have always emphasized their 'Chineseness' and who have created many of the traditions associated with Chinese culture. The Han Chinese spread north, south, east, and west into the many present-day provinces of China, developing their own dialects and cuisines. They now constitute 96 percent of the population.

In the 7th and 14th centuries, imperial expeditions were sent to explore the island of Taiwan and later to repulse Japanese and Okinawan pirates who were using the natural harbors as bases from which to prey on Chinese trading vessels. A migration of farmers and traders began in the 15th century. Most of the immigrants came from two principle groups: the Han Chinese from Fujian province and the Hakkas. 'Hakka' (in Mandarin *Kejya*) refers to a homeless group within China. Much like the Jews in their unsettled history, the Hakkas have wandered throughout China and Southeast Asia in search of a place for themselves. Their name literally means 'guest of the house'. Perhaps they thought they could find a permanent haven for themselves in Taiwan.

The Europeans Arrive

The 16th and 17th centuries saw increased activity in the development of Taiwan. In 1517, the Portugese Admiral Andrade sailed to Taiwan and became so enchanted by the place he named it *Ilha Formosa*, or the 'Beautiful Island'. The Portuguese established a small but important trading presence there.

The Dutch were already established in Indonesia when they sailed north in 1622 and visited the Pescadores (Penghu Islands), a group of small islands between Taiwan and the Chinese mainland. One year later they returned and twisted the Fujian governor's arm to allow them to establish several forts on the island of Taiwan. Forts Zeelandia and Providentia were built from these agreements and the Dutch immediately began to scheme with the aborigines to prepare for greater control. During that period of growing European imperialism, it was inevitable that wherever the Protestant Dutch sailed, the Catholic Spanish would not be far behind. In 1626, the Spanish set up forts in Tamsui and Keelung.

Taiwan was becoming an important entrepôt. It was located right in the middle of what was expected to become a major trading route to Japan. Trade with the Chinese mainland was still conducted offshore, so Taiwan was a door to that market and was a major source for certain valuable commodities like camphor. In 1628, though, the Japanese pulled up their trading outposts and returned to Japan. This may have been ordered by the new Shogunate as part of policies that closed Japan's borders and battened down the hatches for 250 years of isolation.

In 1642, the Dutch, assisted by aborigine warriors, kicked the Spanish off the island. However, major events in China were brewing that would result in the expulsion of the Dutch too. The year 1644 marked the end of the Ming Dynasty, the last of the Han Chinese dynasties. China was taken over by Manchurian horsemen invading from the north, who then created the Qing (Manchu) Dynasty. However, it was not an overnight coup d'état. Countless books, novels, operas, and movies tell how the Ming Loyalists retreated to the south and tried to recapture the empire for their emperor. (The custom of mooncakes is tied up with them, as was the formation of Chinese secret societies.)

One ally of the Loyalists was a rich and influential man known as Koxinga (Jeng Cheng Gung). Koxinga was born to a wealthy Fujian trader and his Japanese wife in 1624. It was said Koxinga's father commanded a fleet of 3,000 sailing vessels and had a business empire that extended into Japan. When Koxinga sided with the Ming Loyalists, he had the power to sail on Taiwan and engage the Dutch in battle. After negotiating their departure in 1662, he established his own state. The resistance to Qing control continued throughout Koxinga's life. His son and grandson eventually took over the reins of power, but in 1683 the resistance was crushed.

For 200 years the Qing authorities paid little heed to Taiwan other than installing a governor and taxing trade in certain commodities. Their political control of Taiwan actually came to be a burden in the gamesmanship played with the European powers, who used any excuse they could find to try to claim damages from the emperor's government. Repayment for damages usually meant forced trading concessions and other shamelessly unequal treaties, which can be read about in more detail in histories of the Opium Wars.

Taiwan was also a burden on China in another way. Its east coast, with its treacherous shores and frequent typhoons, meant that Western traders often lost their ships when navigating this route. The traders could hardly complain to their governments about Taiwan's rugged geography, but when the aborigines began to hunt down and behead the shipwrecked sailors, they had an excuse for action. The British demanded punishment of the aborigines. However, at the time, Taiwan was far from the emperor's mind. He had never been there and could do very little about these non-Chinese mountain people. He demurred. The British would not relent, so he had some aborigines punished. It was not enough and sailors continued to disappear. Finally, a British punitive expedition was sent.

Japanese Colonization

Considering the history of political hassles surrounding Taiwan, it is not surprising that when China was punished by Japan at the end of the First Sino-Japanese War (under the Treaty of Shimonoseki, 1895), the Qing emperor ceded the island to its northern neighbor in perpetuity. There was no discussion with the Taiwanese. The Japanese trumpeted, in a bit of overblown propaganda, that they were finally in possession of the favorite island of their own native son, Koxinga!

A Taiwanese delegation, perhaps at the instigation of the emperor, immediately proclaimed an independent republic. It was doomed to failure. The Japanese landed in Keelung, systematically and quickly fighting their way south.

The Japanese were not kind colonial administrators, but they were efficient. Everything the emperor's government should have been doing and had not was now done by the new masters. It has been commented by historians that Japan had just emerged from its own isolation, was striving to emulate and, as we now know, exceed the West, and wanted to make Taiwan its showcase colony. Roads were built, schools erected, quarantine checkpoints maintained, a railroad line put in, and industries developed. Planned forestry, coal mining, and steel production, not to mention agriculture, all became major industries.

It was the Taiwanese who paid the price for this. Japanese became the medium of instruction in schools; all business with the government had to be conducted in Japanese, even if the clerk was Taiwanese; secret police continued to quash any attempts at Taiwanese independence; Taiwanese conscripts were forced to labor abroad for the Imperial Army; and Taiwanese women were sent to 'comfort' Japanese soldiers. During World War II, Taiwanese conscripts served as far away from home as Manchuria and Indonesia. It was said that when a Taiwanese died during the occupation, he wanted his casket to be taken to the grave under a black umbrella so he would not have to be buried under a Japanese sun.

Meanwhile, events in Mainland China continued to heat up. In 1911, Dr Sun Yat Sen (Swun Jung Shan) overthrew the Manchu Qing Dynasty and in 1912 proclaimed the Republic of China. This led to 38 years of revolution, weakness, strife, massive corruption, cronyism, and untold misery for the Chinese people, until the consolidation of power in 1949 under the Communist leader Mao Tse Tung (Mau Dze Dung). In between, there were constant battles between the Nationalists (the Kuomintang), the warlords, the Communists, and eventually the Japanese during World War II.

A major figure to emerge in China at this time was the leader of the Kuomintang (KMT), Generalissimo Chiang Kai Shek (Jiang Jye Shr). This practiced opportunist married into one of the most powerful families in China. His sister-in-law was Dr Sun's wife, while his other in-laws were the Soongs and the Kungs, among the richest people on the face of the earth. His cultivated connections, assumption of Western airs, and staunchly anti-Communist position won him almost undying support from the United States Congress who, through the years, gave billions of dollars to support his cause. As the KMT army retreated across China, leaving the Chinese people to face horrors at the hands of the Japanese, the U.S. continued to support Chiang. The famous Flying Tigers, an American squadron based in Southwest China, were formed in order to harry Japanese forces with strafing and bombing runs. An air supply route from India to China, 'over the hump' of the Himalayas, was also created.

As the war drew to a close, the United States developed a plan to island-hop to Japan by capturing Taiwan. It was problematic because Taiwan had only three serviceable ports. However, its strategic location and the ability to efficiently supply Chiang while cutting off Japanese supply lines made solid sense. As there were many in the State Department who were leery of Generalissimo Chiang (not so affectionately labelled 'The Gismo' or just 'Peanut' due to his closely shaven head), the island would have been administered as an American trust territory until it could be turned over to a free and organized China. However, the plan was trashed by General MacArthur who, with his vow, "I will return", had promised the Philippines that it would be first on his agenda. So, instead, Taiwan was bombed up and down.

Uncle Sam's Turn

With the surrender of the Japanese on the battleship *Missouri* in August 1945, Taiwan was returned to Chinese sovereignty. The Taiwanese, freed from the yoke of colonial servitude, looked forward to the prospect of membership in a free China. But China was in a shambles! After World War II, Chiang immediately went on the offensive against the Communists, who in turn got support from Stalin. The Chinese people became victims in Chiang's mass scramble to accumulate wealth and Mao's scramble to defeat him. At the same time, it seems that the Kuomintang's view of Taiwan was not very strategic; they believed it was populated by Japanese sympathizers who should be punished by appropriating their property. Chiang sent in one of his less diplomatic generals to do this.

The United States and United Nations officials watched in bewildered horror as the new Nationalist governor systematically alienated the local population of Taiwan. Criticism of Chiang by State Department officials was silenced by Congressional Anti-Communist forces. The situation worsened.

The festering resentment of the local Taiwanese erupted on February 28, 1947, a day for decades whispered about in Taiwan as *Er Er Ba* (2/28, the date the massacre began). Two of Chiang's Tobacco and Wine Monopoly Tax agents approached an old woman street hawker who had some cigarettes and her change before her on a small wooden board. They confiscated her goods and her money and roughed her up. An angry Taiwanese crowd gathered, shots were fired by the taxmen, and six weeks of bloodshed began. All told, it is estimated that 20,000 Taiwanese were killed during this incident. The Governor was recalled, but, following a report discounting the number of deaths, the matter was ordered to be forgotten.

In 1948, however, Taiwan suddenly became more important to the Kuomintang as it dawned on Chiang that it might be his only retreat from China. In another example of his opportunistic genius, he withdrew from the Chinese presidency (with an option to reclaim it at his choice), retired to Taiwan, and diverted U.S. military aid to the island and away from the general he had left in China to fight the Communists. When China fell to the Communists, he could say it was not on his 'watch', reclaim the presidency, and plot his return.

With the victory of Mao's Red Army in Mainland China, two million Mainland Chinese, mainly soldiers and their families, poured across the Straits and into Taiwan. Many of these men were war-weary, ignorant 'grunts' who had nothing and had known nothing but revolution and the corrupt ways of the old regime. They came from far-flung provinces of China, each with its own customs, traditions, and cuisines, and together they spoke a dozen different dialects. The Taiwanese Chinese considered these people interlopers and they resented the uncouth brusqueness they represented, as well as their burden on the island's resources. They were referred to as *Wai Sheng Ren* (People of Foreign Provinces).

Chiang realized several things. His benefactor, the U.S., would no longer support him if he continued to ride roughshod over the local population, allow cronies to stuff their pockets, and not develop the local economy. Without U.S. support his cause was as good as dead. The United Kingdom had already given diplomatic recognition to the People's Republic of China and his faction was losing support in the United Nations. The several hundred thousand soldiers who had retreated from the mainland were unoccupied and unwilling to sit forever without taking action—against him if he was not careful. Moreover, the local population would certainly not put up with the dramatic deterioration in their lifestyle since the defeat of the Japanese without also taking action. Taiwanese politicians who opposed the KMT and were exiled to Japan and the United States began to fight for *Tai Du* (Taiwan Independence), activities that were viciously suppressed by the Kuomintang in Taiwan.

Masterfully, Chiang began to orchestrate the development of Taiwan in moves that were to result in the modern economic miracle people talk about today. Under martial law, Taiwanese business was allowed to flourish and farmlands were redistributed to farmers. Agricultural output increased. Government corporations were created to absorb the excess military personnel. These companies focused on big projects and industries (where it was easier for Chiang and his family cronies to profit), like construction (RSEA), steel (China Steel), shipbuilding (China Shipbuilding), power (Taipower), brewing (Tobacco and Wine Monopoly), sugar (Taisugar), and tourism and travel (China Airlines). These companies became known as *gung jya ji gwan* (public corporations). Tens of thousands of men were thrown into the difficult construction of an east-west scenic highway that served no strategic purpose. Thousands died in landslides and tunnel collapses during its construction. Public schools were built wherein the local population could be indoctrinated in Chinese history and geography, national language, thought, and loyalty, in preparation for recovery of 'the Mainland'. The message was basically: "We can build our prosperity, but dissent from the Kuomintang line will not be tolerated." A political prison was set up on Hungtow where conditions were tough and escape inconceivable.

It should be noted here that, until only several years ago, it was the official line of the Kuomintang government in Taiwan that it was the sole legitimate elected government for the whole of China. Until recently, it was not allowed to publicly or privately question the reality of this stand or to have an election for the national legislature which threatened those aging officials originally elected in the 1940s. Stories were told of such officials attending the sessions in the 1980s in wheelchairs or lying on portable hospital beds with intravenous tubes in their arms!

The Korean War, and more importantly the Vietnam War, were other tremendous supports to Chiang Kai Shek's government. With the U.S. embroiled in anti-Communist battles in Asia, how could they let their old Nationalist friend sink? Massive military, economic, and developmental aid was invested in Taiwan in the 1950s and 60s. Taiwan's economy also benefited from the dollars that came in from

U.S. servicemen sent there for duty or rest and relaxation. B-52 bombing runs on North Vietnam were flown out of Chiang Ching Kuo Airbase in Taichung. There was rapid and balanced economic growth for several decades.

Taiwan On Its Own

Then came several diplomatic blows. First was the 'ping-pong' diplomacy of Henry Kissinger and Richard Nixon when they opened the door to Mainland China, resulting in the Shanghai Communiqué of 1972. The Communiqué was brief, but its intent still influences the relations of China, Taiwan, and the U.S. It was a recognition that Taiwan was a part of China and therefore an internal problem of China. It buried the hopes of *Tai Du* advocates that the U.S. might some day support a free Taiwan. The writing was also on the wall for the Kuomintang. The U.S. recognized the problem as China's and this suggested that U.S. intervention was not to be expected if China attacked Taiwan in an effort to recapture the island.

The second blow was U.S. President Jimmy Carter's breaking of diplomatic relations with the Republic of China (Taiwan) and establishment of relations with the People's Republic of China (Mainland China) in December 1978. Already diplomatically isolated, Taiwan embarked on a path of 'dollar diplomacy'. Ten major infrastructure projects were already nearing completion and more were planned. These improved Taiwan's appearance as an investment site and delivered large contracts to companies in friendly countries.

Taiwan was already a major manufacturing powerhouse for cheap products and the government encouraged investment in factories and industrial upgrading. The New Taiwan Dollar (NT$) was kept at a low value to encourage exports and discourage imports. As a consequence of this, double digit GNP growth was maintained.

The 1980s was an important period of economic, social, and political reform. It began with the maintenance of martial law and

Strategies for Long-Term Stays

Whether it is by insidious design or merely the effect of an imaginative bureaucracy, the visa procedures for foreigners coming to work
and live in Taiwan are difficult and time-consuming to navigate. The
work permit regulations are in a state of flux and, as at the time of
writing, there is much anxiety within the expatriate community in
Taiwan about the prospects.

If you wish to be employed in Taiwan, you will need to apply for
a resident visa and work permit. This can only be done by first getting
approvals from 'appropriate government departments' in Taiwan and
then making an application at a consulate or official office abroad, not
in Taiwan. You must leave to make the application and even then the
visa is very hard to get.

This is and has been the policy for a long time, so why the anxiety
of the expatriate community? Because many expats have through the
years skirted these regulations. There are many foreigners who have
ostensibly lived and worked in Taiwan for years, even decades,
without resident visas, work permits, and without paying taxes. They
are not just maids. Hundreds of Westerners taught English or ran
trading companies this way. So, how did they do it? They simply
renewed their 60-day visitor visa twice and at the end of every six
months they would take a brief vacation (sometimes as brief as the one
hour needed to get on the next plane back!) in Hong Kong, Seoul, or
Manila, only to return and renew the six-month cycle. Sometimes
whole families would do this. Now, however, the government is
finally cracking down, with the result that lots of foreigners are
scurrying for cover.

The government is trying to replace the old convoluted and
protectionist system with one that encourages honesty. The new rules
are so new that expats are not sure how efficiently or fairly they will
be enforced.

Therefore, the best solution in trying to secure your long-term stay
is to pursue the open way first. Your prospective employer in Taiwan

will have to help you and your family to apply for the resident visa and work permit approval at the 'appropriate government department' and then at the Ministry of Foreign Affairs. When approval is granted, you can then make an application to the consulate abroad.

If you are hoping to reside but not work in Taiwan, the best alternative is to enrol in a language course at an institution recognized by the government. You can then get a resident permit based on your student status. This does not allow you to legally work. You will need to travel abroad once more to get your resident visa processed.

Within 15 days of your arrival with your resident visa, you must still go to the Foreign Service Center of the police and apply for your alien resident certificate. Before you depart Taiwan for business or pleasure, you must apply for an exit permit. This normally takes two to three days to process.

Visas and Business Law

The changes in immigration procedures recently promulgated also touch the following areas, which are structural rather than procedural. Residence or work permits, along with alien resident certificates and overseas applications are all still required:

- *Foreign Investment-Approved and Foreign Branch Companies.* If your employer in Taiwan fits this category, the issuance of work permits to foreigners has been relaxed. The employer must no longer demonstrate that certain capital or income requirements have been met.
- *Capital and Income Tests.* In order to be eligible to hire foreign workers (i.e. get approved work permits) companies must meet certain minimum requirements. If it is a local company its capital must exceed NT$5 million. If it is a branch of a foreign company, then the figure is NT$2.5 million. Companies set up less than one year need not demonstrate income to apply for a work permit. If set up over one year, they must demonstrate an average income exceeding NT$10 million per annum. Trading companies must

demonstrate average annual imports and exports exceeding U.S.$1 million or commissions on trading exceeding US$400,000.

- *The Long-Term Resident.* If you have managed to stay in Taiwan continuously for five years with 'good behavior' (no one is sure whether this means that you have not been engaging in black market employment) you will have the right to a work permit.

If this seems too mind-numbing a way to secure a work permit, then you might turn to your company's accounting firm. Most international accounting firms maintain consultancies which can provide assistance in wading through the bureaucracy...for a fee. The Asia Enterprise Center has also been reporting on the new immigration regulations for *This Month in Taiwan* magazine. They can provide further information and assistance. Contact John Weston on telephone (886-2)7195008 or facsimile (886-2)7176088.

CUSTOMS AND IMMIGRATION

Once you have secured the necessary visa and are finally on the plane to Taiwan, you will probably be given a three-part form. This is used both for immigration and customs. It should be filled out in pen prior to getting in line. At the airport, immigration counters do not distinguish between Republic of China and foreign passport holders, so you can line up at any counter.

From immigration you proceed to pick up your baggage at the carousel. At Chiang Kai Shek International Airport there are free trolleys to use—the worst in Asia! Woe to the businessman who takes his trolley before getting his luggage and puts his heavily laden attaché case or duty free liquor into the wire basket designed to hold it. The trolley immediately flips over, crashing the business case or bottles to the floor. Also, please note, the wheels were put on backwards. The design semantics tell you to push the cart, but they are best pulled rather than pushed.

At customs there are three categories of inspectors: those for Taiwanese, those for diplomats, and those for foreign passport holders. You must produce your passport and the customs form that the immigration officer folded into your passport, and then put your bags up on the counter for inspection. Unlike other more relaxed countries in Asia, in Taiwan you will not be waved through without some scrutiny. Sometimes they open all your bags, sometimes only one.

On the customs form you should note anything exceptional that you are carrying. A list of restricted items is available from the customs, but needless to say the carrying of weapons, illicit drugs, and pornography will result in big trouble. Printed matter from Mainland China or anything which is critical of Taiwan might be confiscated, though this has been relaxed considerably. Gold bullion and large quantities of currency must be declared or it can be confiscated. Report the approximate amount of currency you are carrying. You do not have to account for every penny. If, however, you are carrying more than NT$40,000 (around U.S.$1,600 at the time of writing) you are required to have a permit from the Ministry of Finance. Carry your allocated purchases of duty free liquor and tobacco conspicuously to avoid delays.

There is a section of the form devoted to unaccompanied baggage. If you have household items being shipped separately that are already en route, check with your moving company for procedures. They may want you to attach a bill of lading or declaration onto your customs form.

Also, if you want to leave some items at the airport or if the customs officer wants to hit you for duty on something you can temporarily live without, you can put the item in storage before going through the customs. Do not lose the receipt and allow sufficient time when you depart Taiwan for the airline to claim it from customs and put it on the plane for you.

TRANSPORT FROM THE AIRPORT

Kaohsiung Airport is located at the edge of the city and if you are going to a hotel there, a taxi is your best option. From Chiang Kai Shek International, though, it is best to weigh your options. The bigger hotels maintain a limousine service which can meet you and take you right away to your hotel. If your company has a presence in Taiwan already, they may have special rates for this service with the hotel. Book through your company as this is otherwise the most expensive option. Taxis are also expensive, usually about U.S.$48 to the city. There is not an orderly queue. Cabbies may try to hustle you into their car. Ask for the price before you get in the cab. Occasionally you can arrange to share.

There is a convenient bus service from Chiang Kai Shek International. Right after leaving the customs area, immediately turn left and walk to the end of the building. There are two lines waiting to board the buses for Taipei. Buy your ticket first at a window to the right of the boarding area. The current price to Taipei is NT$83 (around U.S.$3.32). There are two choices of bus. One bus goes to the Miramar Hotel and Sung Shan Domestic Airport in the northeastern quadrant of the city. The other bus goes to the Santos Hotel and the Taipei Railway Station at the west and center of the city. Pick the best one according to your ultimate destination. Get in the correct line and when it is time to depart, you will be asked to put your bags beneath or on the bus, depending on your destination. Do not expect a receipt for your luggage. Buses depart every quarter hour and the air-conditioned ride takes 45 to 60 minutes. From the downtown drop-off point you can easily get a cab to your destination, usually for less than U.S.$8. There is a similar bus service to Hsinchu (Syinju).

Unlike in some other Asian countries, foreign exchange counters at the airports in Taiwan offer fair rates for exchanging your currency. However, travellers should note that there is not the black market for U.S. dollars that existed 15 years ago.

RESTING YOUR HEAD

It has been a long flight and a long day. You will be glad you made the arrangements for your accommodations before you arrived. You didn't? In that case, when you come out of the customs area walk straight across the lobby to a row of hotel representatives. This is not the best place to make a booking as you cannot negotiate with them and the choice, though ample, is limited to those larger hotels that can afford (because of their rates) to have a representative at the airport. Alternatively, you can lug your baggage downtown, make some phone calls, and hope for the best.

Taipei has a growing stable of first-class, international 'name brand' hotels. These are located in banking and business districts, have good but absurdly expensive restaurants, and cater to your every whim with business centers, pools, health spas, and concierge who speak your language. Be prepared to spend at least U.S.$200 per night for the pillow. Breakfast will set you back another U.S.$20. There are also some homegrown five-star hotels. Staying with them will save you 10 percent, but you will probably get a 10-percent reduction in amenities as well. A tax and service charge will inflate your bill another 23 percent at all 'nice' hotels.

Between four-star and no-star hotels is a sliding scale of price and quality. Prices range from U.S.$140 for a single room, down to U.S.$40, including breakfast. Rooms will come with bath, TV, and air-conditioning.

Besides hotels there are the 'rest houses' which rent by the hour for couples who want to get away from the in-laws. These rooms are also available for the night, but cash-in-advance payment is required and no breakfast is served. They are usually decorated for sexual adventure: mirrored ceilings, round beds, lacy this and that, and a lot of pink. If you are not carrying valuables (which might be stolen) and are on a tight budget, the price range of U.S.$20–45 per night may interest you. These are not brothels, though you may indeed receive a phone call soliciting interest as they are frequently located in 'entertainment' areas of the city.

Also in this price range are the various guesthouses, YMCA and such. Prices are quite reasonable, but the availability of rooms is usually limited. Try to make the necessary arrangements before you arrive in Taiwan.

If you are travelling on a budget you will be blessed if you have a friend already living in Taiwan on whom you can impose yourself for a few days. This will allow you the greatest of luxuries: saving money while learning about the country from someone in a similar situation to yourself. A week in such circumstances would be worth a month searching for your own options. One such option might be to stay long-term in a Buddhist monastery. This would, of course, represent the most fully-immersed, yet severe lifestyle possible for a foreigner. The authors are aware of only one person who had the guts to do this in Taiwan, but she was a fluent Mandarin-speaker and Chinese physician!

SURVIVING YOUR FIRST IMPRESSIONS

Unless you come from some worse place like Chernobyl, Beirut or New York City, then your first impressions of Taipei will more than likely be unfavorable. Even though Chris had studied Chinese language and culture for two years before coming to Taiwan, he still found much of what awaited him to be discomfiting. Many daunting 'first impression' images come to mind: traffic congestion, noisy diners, red and seemingly tubercular expectorations dotting the sidewalks (betel nut juice), air pollution, a garnish of Western values. All these are apparent on the surface and if you do not look beyond what is apparent, you will miss the beauty, simplicity, cultural depth, and kindness that do exist here. To a certain extent, that is the purpose of this book: to guide you in what to expect and what to look for, so you can survive your first impressions and get onto the good parts. Read thoroughly, keep your eyes open for the good things that happen around you, and be patient.

Chapter Three

SETTLING IN

If you are moving to Taiwan to work or study, you will want to find permanent accommodation quickly. If your company is transferring you and your family, it is wise to ask for a house-hunting trip. This will allow you and your spouse a chance to look at the local situation clearly before making the big move. It will also allow you to arrange for accommodation prior to packing and moving, understand better what things to bring and what to leave behind, give you a chance to get the work permit application prepared if necessary, and will help to minimize the time you spend in a hotel after you arrive. There are, however, some service apartments and 'residence inn' type hotels which offer a mid-term alternative while looking for your own place.

THE RIGHT PLACE FOR YOU

Before trying to find a real estate agent, it would probably be wise to tour the city, get the lay of the land, understand where your office is, where schools and recreation are located, and what types of areas cater to people with your budget. If people from your own company or expatriate friends could accompany you on this tour, all the better. Ultimately, only you know how close you need to be to the foreign community support net, how much short commutes mean to you, etc. In this chapter the focus is on Taipei, since that is where most expatriates wind up. However, if you are destined for Hsinchu, Taichung, or Kaohsiung it would still be useful to read on.

A Tour of the Taipei Area

Your driving tour of the areas around Taipei might go like this:

1. Start the day with a drive up **Yangmingshan**. This is a mountain to the north of Taipei, popular with the wealthiest locals and expatriates. Here you will pass many private villas, all with yards or gardens, some with their own swimming pools or tennis courts. The air is relatively fresh, the homes spacious, the view desirable, and the prices astronomical. Shopping is not particularly available, nor is access to schools, though the American Club, is not too far away.

2. Drive down the opposite side of Yangmingshan to **Wellington Heights**. This is an old community built up on a quiet and green hillside, for the most part facing away from Taipei. Prices are slightly less than Yangmingshan for stand-alone houses. Since the area is secluded, public transport is infrequent and taxi drivers grumble about going all the way up the hill to drop or pick up passengers.

3. Next stop is Tienmu. On the way to Tienmu you will pass through **Shihpai**. This is primarily a Chinese community, though some

foreigners may spill over into it. It will certainly become a more attractive alternative upon the completion of the Taipei Mass Rapid Transit system (MRT) which will go through Shihpai. The unofficial demarcation line between Shihpai and Tienmu is the stream just beyond Veteran's Hospital.

4. **Tienmu** is all the way at the end of Chungshan North Road, half an hour north of the city. It is the most conspicuous foreign ghetto. Here you will find the Taipei American and Japanese schools, and the Taipei Youth Program Association (a foreign youth community center). Small grocery shops here have been stocking strange foreign brand goods for decades. Some larger local supermarkets have also moved in. The bus terminus for Chungshan Road is part of the heart of this suburban city. It makes public transport readily accessible. Taxis are also fairly easy to get.

Tienmu is convenient for schooling, socializing, shopping, and living. There is a wide variety of housing, from high-rise apartments packed in alleys, to smaller villas on the side of hills, to ground floor walk-in units in small side streets. Prices vary widely. Air quality is better than Taipei but not as good as Yangmingshan. If your office is in Taipei, count on an hour to get to work, or double if you take a bus and need to change lines downtown.

5. Between Tienmu and Taipei is **Shihlin**. This used to be a local enclave, but has grown by leaps and bounds in recent years. The Taipei French, English, and German schools are located here. The MRT will have a stop in Shihlin. It borders on Taipei, yet is not too far from the foreign schools, and the prices are better than downtown. The air quality begins to deteriorate the closer you get to the city.

6. Far on the other side of the city is a rapidly growing area with many new apartment complexes, popular with wealthy, trendy, and young Chinese and expatriates. It is the **Chunghsiao East** and **Jenai Road** areas. This is a location for people who like to be in the middle of everything and probably do not have school-age children. It is

convenient for entertainment, shopping, and many of the major modern office complexes that have sprung up here and on Dunhwa Road.

7.   Of course, if you are adventurous, on a very tight budget, or your primary purpose in coming to Taiwan was to learn about the language and culture, then you can really look anywhere. Having a car also widens the horizons. The Taipei city folk are expanding out across the rivers to **Lujou**, **Yungho**, and **Hsindian**. Take a look at these suburbs if you require more reasonably priced local living in new apartments and don't mind a considerable commute.

A Note on Locations

Volcanic fissures are abundant in Taiwan and have created the many soothing hot mineral springs people enjoy here. However, in northern Taipei especially, they add a heavy mineral content to both the air and public water supply. This rapidly and thoroughly tarnishes silver, silver plate, and lower carats of gold. Unless you enjoy polishing silver, have a maid to help, or must bring your silver set for business entertaining, then we suggest you either leave it at home or move to a different part of the city.

Buy, Rent or Share?

Taiwan real estate prices have been growing rapidly. Fortunes have been made and lost in land speculation in Taiwan. If you have a fat bank account and a taste for risk, you might consider buying an apartment. The prices are high compared to almost anywhere else in the world, but if you are already from a major city or capital, you won't find them too daunting. Shop around carefully for the right area, compare prices, and understand that you will most probably have to pay cash.

Renting is the option most people pursue. If you are interested in sharing, you can put a notice up in the American and other foreign clubs, in *The China Post* and *China News* (the two local English language newspapers), and at the many larger English cram schools

37

where lesser-paid English and American expatriates tend to hang out.

The Real Estate Agent

This profession has a perhaps deserved reputation worldwide for being less trustworthy than the average citizen. In Taiwan, real estate agents are no different, but the rules of the game are new to you. The real estate problem in any country is the question of whom the agent acts for and how much they are obliged to disclose. In Taiwan, the agent receives commissions from both the landlord and the tenant. Keep your own interests in mind and speak to the agent as if they are the landlord. Do not 'show your hand', and do not let them know that your 'company is paying the whole bill and you just want to find a great place, to hell with the cost!'

If you look for rental apartments and agents only in the classifieds of the two papers mentioned above, you are sure to get stuck with only the most expensive expat-targeted units to view. Nevertheless, if you have not learned any Mandarin yet and have no one to help you with translation, these English-speaking agents may be your only recourse. It does not hurt, though, to shop around. Once you have selected a suitable location to live in, find a real estate agent in that part of the city. The hotel concierge or your office staff can help you here. Ask them to call to see if the agency has any English speakers; you may get lucky. Also remember that the more specific you can be about what is most important to you and your family, the better. Before you meet with the agent, try to decide on the relative importance of the following:

- **Proximity** to
  - Schools
  - Expat shopping
  - Work
  - Entertainment and recreation
- **Environment**
  - Spacious or small
  - Green
  - Suburban
  - High-rise
  - Detached house
  - Urban
- **Price**
  - No limit
  - Budget
  - No budget
- **Others**
  - Car park space
  - Security

In Taiwan, landlords may demand six, 12, or even 24 months' rent in advance from expatriates. For so much up-front cash, it is important that you like what you get. It is also important to negotiate completely with the landlord any necessary structural changes or improvements before you place a deposit. Painting, woodwork, sanitary fixtures, lighting, air-conditioning, security systems, additional power points, satellite TV reception, kitchen equipment, and cabinets might all be subject to negotiation and renovation depending on the rental price and terms. The contract should specifically detail the required improvements, the quality of materials, who is responsible for what level of repair after you have taken over the property, who pays for supplementary expenses (guard, parking space, etc.), and the conditions of the deposit return at the end of the lease. Contracts should be in English and Chinese.

Landlords are generally willing to accommodate renovations, but in return expect a long-term commitment from the tenant. Only place a fraction of the final payment (perhaps one month's rent) with the landlord or agent on signing the contract and reserve the remainder until all the work is done to your satisfaction. Expect the agent to help you negotiate, but do not let them know what your 'final offer' is until you reach that point and keep yourself fully involved in the negotiation. Expect the agent to 'ride shotgun' on the landlord to see that he honors all the terms and conditions of renovation.

Ping-Pong

The unit of measurement for floor area in houses, apartments, and offices is the *ping*. Imported from Japan (where it is called the *tsubo*), the *ping* corresponds to the floor area occupied by two woven straw *tatami* mats, an area which covers approximately 36 square feet. An advertisement might say, "48 ping, expat quality apartment, 3 bedrooms", which means that that the square footage is about 1,728.

Home Appliances

Standard wall voltage in Taiwan is 110V and most appliances from America will operate without a problem. So, if you have a favorite pasta-maker, bread-baker, waffle iron, or other unusual appliance of this voltage it is safe to bring it with you. Most homes also have a limited number of 220V sockets for plugging in air-conditioners, so other voltage appliances could possibly be used.

Remember that Chinese cuisine includes very little baking. A typical 'expat' apartment may be equipped with a range that has an oven, but a local apartment certainly will not. Know your budget, tour prospective homes before you move, and find out what you will need to bring from home. Certainly bring your baking pans, crockery and Western utensils, as it is unlikely you will find exact replacements of your favorite kitchen equipment.

Getting Domestic Help

Taiwan is not the paradise it once was for expatriates, who could previously afford the luxury of a driver, houseboy, gardener, and amah/cook. The standard of living has increased so rapidly, and across the whole of society, that it is indeed difficult to find people to work as domestic help. If you are intending to hire a full-time, English-speaking, Taiwanese maid, you are probably on a full-blown expatriate benefits package, but you must be prepared to spend considerable time finding the rare person who will be willing to work for you. There are, however, several full-time and part-time alternatives.

The first is to hire an 'imported' maid, as increasing numbers of affluent Taiwanese do themselves. Most of these workers are women who come from the Philippines. The plus is that they can speak English fairly well. The downside (and it is a big one if you yourself are new to Taiwan) is that unless you hire a Filipina already experienced in working in Taiwan, these girls will be suffering the same culture shock that you are (maybe even worse). They will not be able to shop, communicate with neighbors, or run errands any better than you can. The other downside is that to legally employ such a maid is a time-consuming, fully bureaucratized task. Call the Council of Labor Affairs on 7182512 for details on current regulations. To hire an illegal Filipina amah (no working papers) can subject you to fines if she is caught. We understand that the government has cracked down on these workers, so consider whom you employ very carefully.

Alternatively, hire a part-time maid. Both Taiwanese and Filipinas perform these services. The best place to start looking is through friends, referrals, and bulletin boards. The latter are maintained at some grocery stores serving the expatriate community in Tienmu and at clubs like the American Club. Expatriate families moving away will frequently put up a notice trying to help a trusted maid find a new employer.

Handling Domestic Help

Remember that a maid will have access to everything in your house and might be entrusted with your children's safety. Referrals or a discussion with the previous employer is strongly recommended. During the interview, explain fully what responsibilities, hours, time off, privileges, meals, holidays, and rules are expected of the candidate, so you can determine if there is any resistance. If you expect the amah to help take care of the children, then it is best to have your kids meet her to gauge their acceptance. Finally, when you have made a selection, make up a weekly schedule of what is to be done and when. During the first week help the maid understand how you want things to be done.

It is a good idea to agree in advance on a one-month trial period, during which time both parties can get to know one another. If this is your first overseas assignment, it is possible that this is also your first household help. Adjusting to managing the house rather than doing it yourself can be a shock (whatever you may think about housework!). Understand that this may be the result of your own frustration in dealing with the maid and don't blame everything on her. However, if either party finds the work unacceptable, pay for the number of days worked and resume your search. If after the one month trial things turn sour, make a determination quickly and settle the matter with surgical immediacy. Make sure keys are returned and then change the locks. Be prepared to pay severance of five percent of the total salary paid to date. Despite having to ask the maid to leave, be as positive as possible about the termination to preserve the 'face' of the employee (for more about 'face', see Chapter Five).

If you are fortunate enough to have a yard, you may need to hire a gardener to help you. Maids do not do outside work. When looking for a gardener, you should follow the procedures outlined above.

SHOPPING

The routine of going out to procure the daily necessities of life can either be a frustrating and disgusting experience, or else a source of adventure, amusement, and cultural awakening. Most Westerners who venture to Taiwan will have been raised in a relatively sterile, pasteurized, processed, packaged-for-convenience, fixed-price world. Meats, for instance, have no relation to the animal they came from by the time we see them. They are filleted, breaded, cubed, ground, marinated. We are divorced from the source of our foods, the smell of anything but fresh meats and vegetables, and the rigors of bargaining for even small items.

Taiwan is a land of entrepreneurs. It is almost everyone's wish to be their own boss, to have a pushcart, stall, restaurant, shop, company, or major corporation all their own. In Taipei a walk down almost any avenue, street, lane, or alley will take you past shop after shop after shop. The sequence of these small shops might go like this: cafeteria, stationery, pharmacy, clothing store, bakery, convenience, tire, hardware, video, clinic, repeat, repeat. Inside the stationer's you can get newspapers, pens, all manner of paper and envelopes, file folders, and usually some little toys and sports equipment. Occasionally they also sell stamps. The bakery will sell milk and soft drinks. The clothing store may sell fish from dawn to 10 a.m. Welcome to the real world of shopping in Taiwan!

Though the modernization of consumer retailing is rapidly changing the way the Taiwanese shop, there are still many opportunities to enjoy the 'traditional' shopping experience. The *Yellow Pages* in Taiwan are in Chinese, so your fingers won't walk very far here! Looking at the various guidebooks on Taiwan can provide you with the addresses of shops that sell the items you want. Copy the Chinese address down, or take the book along, and carry the phone number in case you get lost. An easier option is to make friends with local people who can show you around their favorite shopping haunts.

The Art of Bargaining

Because they are their own boss, the Taiwanese entrepreneur can make decisions about prices and terms of sale right on the spot. This facilitates the 'culture of negotiation' in Taiwan. The art of the negotiated purchase is ancient and venerated here. Much zest is injected by the Taiwanese into any major acquisition by the thrust and parry of bargaining. Some Westerners from certain countries and cultures are more equipped than others to readily mesh with the bargaining scene in Taiwan. Nevertheless, there are some unwritten ground rules of the game to keep in mind:

1. Always start at a price lower than the price at which you expect to get the item.
2. Know as much as possible about what you are getting and its relative value before going into the final negotiation. The merchant will respect the knowledgeable opponent and making outlandishly low offers or extravagant claims will insult the art.
3. Keep your cool when negotiating. There is really nothing about which to get uptight. Smile with a firmly resolved face. Threats will not help.
4. Remember there are things besides cash to be negotiated: delivery, installation, and accessories should be included in the bargaining.

A Bargaining Encounter

So, you have decided to purchase a television and you have been to three stores to check the price of brand X model Y. You return to the shop that quoted the lowest and tell the shopkeeper you want to ask about the price again. He quotes you the same price. Ask what that includes. He indicates that it includes an antenna, a remote control, and a one-year manufacturer's warranty. "What about delivery?" you ask. "Where do you live?" he asks. You tell him and he agrees. Now, tell him you are willing to pay the price less 15%. He makes a large groan and grimaces, maybe smiles, shakes his head, but refuses. "What is your best cash price?" you ask. "Price less 5%," he replies. Offer price less 10%. He refuses. Ask if he can include some video cassette tapes or a VCR hook-up cable. He agrees. Offer the price less 7.5%. He refuses. Ask him when he closes for the night, then make an effort to leave. He may stop you. If not, keep walking. Go back to store number two and try to get better than the price less 5%. If the manager of store number one does ask you to stop, then smile and say you really want to buy it with cash right now and you are just asking for 2.5% discount (the price less 5% is now the established price from your point of view). He may now agree.

Where and When to Bargain

With the advent of Western-style retailing, where and when to bargain on prices has become clouded. About 20 years ago, some shops began displaying signs that read *Bu Er Jya* (No Second Price, in other words, Fixed Price Shop). The shop owners' hope was to stop eroding margins by claiming that they would not countenance bargaining. However, most of them would lower the price if the purchase was right or if a local was buying, so the signs were largely ignored.

Now, though, with Western-style convenience and department stores, bargaining is definitely out. You could still try in other large stores, if you have the guts, but we can't guarantee the reaction of the store assistant. Some shops, like the occasional bookstore, might give you a discount, even if you do not ask! Below is a guide (that is by no means complete) which serves to demonstrate the trickiness of this question.

Item or Type of Shop	When Bargaining is Accepted
Automobile	Required
House Rental	Required
Major Appliance	Required at small shops. At larger retailers, negotiate for extras.
Small Appliance	Acceptable at small shops, not at larger retailers.
Restaurants	Never, unless preparing for a banquet.

Hotels	Room rates can be negotiated prior to checking in.
Repair Services	Acceptable
Supermarket	Unacceptable
Department Store	Unacceptable
Small 'Mom & Pop' Shops	Acceptable if the purchase is above NT$1,000.
Small Specialty Retailers	These might be selling shoes, clothes, toys, hardware, lighting, art, antiques. Acceptable for purchases of over NT$1,000.
Street Vendors	Acceptable, except with food vendors.

A final word about bargaining. If you have finally managed to get the vendor down to the price you want and then whip out your American Express card, you will leave for home without it (the purchase that is!). Credit cards charge one to three percent to vendors for purchases made with a card. Either be prepared to pay cash, tell the man up front at the beginning that you intend to pay by card, or allow him to put the several percent charge on top of the purchase price.

Groceries

You have four choices in buying your groceries. These are listed below, with comments about their relative convenience and expense.

- **Home Delivery and Import Grocery Stores.** The medium-sized grocery stores in expatriate enclaves have delivery services. This is both convenient and costly. They charge you the same price as if you bought at the store, but it is more expensive because, unless you specify the brand, they buy the more expensive imported label for you. These are the stores you will have to patronize to get specialty items for seasonal expatriate use, like turkey roasting pans and stuffing, for example.
- **Convenience Stores** (7-11, Nikko Mart, President Bakeries,

Family Mart, etc.). These stores have spread like termites throughout the major cities, eating away at and displacing the 'mom and pop' shops. Their opening hours are great and, while they sell many different types of items, you often find that there is only one or two of each thing on the shelf. Prices are also about 10 percent higher than elsewhere.

- **Supermarkets.** Smaller than their Western cousins, these are still 'super' on the Taiwanese scale. They carry a complete selection of fresh and packaged goods, meats, and dry goods. Prices tend to be fair and stable. But note that locally-made packaged goods from these supermarkets will probably not have English labeling.

- **Vegetable Markets** (*Tsai Shr Chang*). This category deserves special attention on its own. For obvious reasons, other parts of Chinese-speaking Asia refer to these as 'wet markets'. If you go to one, do not dress up or wear a nice pair of white shoes. The concrete floor is frequently wet, either with rinse water or the effluent of raw foods (blood, slime, scales, etc.). Be prepared for a smell like nothing you have smelled in the grocery store at home. It is worth getting used to, though, for this is where the Taiwanese traditionally shop for all their food needs on a daily basis. This is where you and your children can be given free street courses in biology, dissection, vivisection, and animal anatomy. It is also where the full bounty of Taiwan's fields, orchards, streams, and seas is on display in all its freshness and glory. These market areas are usually set up by the government and the stalls are rented out to vendors who take the same spot every day with their fresh produce. Let's walk through a typical market.

A Stroll Through the Wet Market

You will enter from the sidewalk, usually into a poorly lit area of rows and rows of small stands. Each stand usually comprises a table, around 10 feet by 5 feet, that has an array of goods displayed on it. Vegetable vendors are lined up together. Their tables might display

many different kinds of leafy vegetables, for example cabbage (*baitsai,* a k a *bakchoy*), heartless vegetable (*kungsyin tsai*), or Chinese broccoli (*gailan*). Alternatively, the stall might specialize, selling only garlic or chillies or sweet potatoes.

The meat vendors are also together; beef here, pork there, cooked chicken and duck at another stall. But do not come here to buy a New York-cut sirloin steak or, indeed, any recognizable cut of meat, beyond pork chops (*paigu*). The Taiwanese use limited beef in their cuisine and do not use cuts that will be familiar to you. At the pork stall, you can see whole heads, sides, legs, and accessories. Taiwanese pork is fresh and excellent, and you can get ribs, chops, and loins. Only 25 years ago, in poorer times, the only meat many people could afford on a regular basis was sow's ears. Times have changed.

At one stand you can buy fresh chickens—very fresh. Inside rows of cages are live pullets and roosters, clucking and crowing about. You can select a regular chicken or a *tuji* (literally 'earth chicken', i.e. range chicken) which Chinese chefs and nutritionists prefer. Don't worry

49

about having to pluck the feathers. Pick out the chicken you want and the vendor will put it into what Chris calls the 'Wonderful Chicken-Stripping Machine'. The vendor will remove the chicken from the cage and deftly slit its throat. While being drained of life it is put into a device that looks like a spin washer. It is a stainless steel barrel with rubber nails lining its internal surface. When the motor engages, the chicken bounces about inside at high speed (bing-bing-bong-bong!) while the vendor pours a scupper of boiling hot water onto the bird. Forty-five seconds later a denuded bird emerges. The vendor will clean the guts out for you and give you the bird (head, claws, and all), still at body temperature, in a plastic bag.

In the seafood section you will see very fresh whole fish, squid, octopus, crustaceans, and shellfish on beds of ice. Pick out what you want. A fish will be gutted and scaled while you wait, but will still be delivered to you complete with head. Note that vendors charge you for the weight of the whole fish before gutting, even if you ask them to cut off and discard the head. However, the fishmonger only charges according to the weight of the selected piece for choice cuts like a swordfish steak.

Then there are the soybean curd vendors. Bean curd, known in the West by its Japanese name *tofu,* is called *doufu* in Mandarin. Chris refers to it as 'The Cheese of the Chinese' since bean curd truly fulfills the nutritional requirements in the Chinese diet that dairy products fill in the West. It is also just as versatile. Most Westerners know bean curd as a whitish, soft, flavorless, custard-like substance. It is made from ground soybeans and water.

The Taiwanese eat *doufu* in many different ways, depending on how much moisture is removed. As a soup (full water), it is called *dou jiang* (bean sauce). Fermented *dou jiang* is called *dou jr* (bean juice). Thicken and ferment it in a different way and you have Japanese *miso* paste, used as a flavoring and fortifier for a number of dishes. With the water squeezed out, it becomes large slab-like cakes. These are cut up and sold in smaller cakes. If it is extruded now it becomes *doufu sz* (bean curd threads). If it is marinated and dried further, it becomes *doufu gan* (dried bean curd). If it is fermented, it becomes *chou doufu* (smelly bean curd). If it is deep fried it becomes *ja doufu* (fried bean curd). Dried in sheets it is called *doufu pi* (bean curd skin).

At the vegetable market you can also buy prepared foods: roasted chickens and ducks, barbecued sausages, pickled and salted vegetables, roasted peanuts and peanut candy, dried fruits and fish, etc.

Slim Jins

Supermarkets and convenience stores use the metric system for weighing goods and packaged foods. However, at the traditional market, the Chinese weights and measures system is based on the *jin*, for some obscure reason called the 'catty' in English. A comparison chart of the various metric, imperial and Chinese weights is listed below.

1 *jin*	=	1.32 lbs
1 lb	=	0.75 *jin*
1 kg	=	2.2 lbs
1 kg	=	1.66 *jin*
100 g	=	3.52 oz
1 *jin*	=	0.6 kg

Goods in the vegetable markets are sold either by units (for example, four oranges for NT$100) or by weight (NT$30 for 1 *jin*). Many displays of produce have signs made with scraps of cardboard and felt-tip pens that indicate how goods are priced each day. If you do not see a sign, ask before you have the vendor load up the bag or cut the meat to your requirements. The question to ask is, "*Yi jin dwo shau chyan?*" (How much is one *jin*?).

Generally, you cannot bargain at the vegetable markets. There are, however, many vendors of any particular item and we encourage you to spend your first day perusing the merchandise, asking how much, how much, and 'comparison shopping'. Some will let you squeeze and smell the merchandise, but some will be fussy and could complain if you do. Once you've familiarized yourself, settle on a group of vendors who will get to know you, know how you want your fish prepared, your ribs chopped, your pineapple shucked— whatever your pleasure. They will begin to anticipate your patronage and look forward to seeing you, even helping you to pick out the sweeter or juicier stock.

No White Sales

One thing you will not readily find around the shops and markets in Taiwan are the 'white sales' common in the West. Even department stores do not stock up on the kind and quality of sheets, towels, and rugs that you are probably used to. Bring a supply of towels with you and, since mattresses are of a slightly different size in Taiwan, it is best to bring your own bed and mattress if you can afford to. If you are using a local bed, it is still best to bring sheets from home and alter them, if necessary, to fit. Custom-made and sized mattresses are an alternative that some expats have resorted to. Know the exact size of your mattress back home before you commit to this, then you can be sure the sheets you bring with you will fit. Imported sheets and pillow cases are expensive. If you like a warm bed on a cold winter night, don't forget the electric blanket!

Clothes

Dress standards depend on the industry or business you are in. In many offices, suits are rarely seen and a shirt and tie is sufficient. Leisure suits and sports jackets are popular with locals. But please note that Taipei and most of Taiwan has four seasons. Though this is a 'tropical island' you would not know it in the middle of a cold and dreary Taipei evening in February. Most homes and many offices are not heated. This means you will need lots of layers of clothing, but probably not the heavy, winter sort which will make you overheat.

During the hot humid summers from mid-May to mid-September (often 32 degrees centigrade, 90 percent humidity), you will need light cotton clothes. The spring and autumn periods are usually warm and pleasant, but the cool dreary winters in February and March (17 degrees centigrade, 80 percent humidity) require woolens, underwear of natural fibres (which allow your skin to breath under warmer clothes), sweaters, and flannel.

The Ubiquitous T-Shirt

Taiwanese men will almost always have a singlet or T-shirt on under their polo or business shirt. This applies even in the summer, especially if working in an air-conditioned office. Chinese medical theory warns against sweating and being subjected to drafts. After many summer colds, Chris adopted this custom of wearing a minimum of two layers of clothing all year round. Sure enough, we saw the colds and sinus problems vanish, without an increase in heat discomfort or body odor.

Buying Clothes

Imported clothes and fashions are not cheap in Taiwan, despite the fact that many clothes are made here. Although the Yves St. Laurent shirt you bought on sale in America or London for U.S.$25 ironically has a 'Made in Taiwan' label inside it, you will not readily find that one for sale here in the place it was made. These are usually for export only and if you do find and buy one in Taiwan, you will pay no less than US$55— the 'imported' cost!

Moreover, the clothes that you do find locally (priced reasonably or not) will probably not fit, unless you are sized and shaped like the average Taiwanese. Chris' martial arts master was a sizable five feet six inches and weighed 200 lbs. Hard-pressed to get clothes locally, he had a standing request with Chris to bring him shirts, sweaters, and windbreakers from overseas. Most expatriates have to do the same. Stock up before you come. You should include underwear, T-shirts, shirts, slacks, shoes (besides sneakers), and suits. The more formal the item, the less likely they will have your size and the higher the price.

Tailoring in Taiwan is a possibility. It might still be cheaper than having clothes tailored in the West, but Hong Kong is a better bet if you want to have several suits and a dozen shirts made up in one hit. There is a greater availability of larger sizes there too. Some expats make shopping trips to Hong Kong just for this.

If you still need or want to shop for clothes in Taiwan, your best bet will be casual and sports clothes. Hit the streets and scour the stalls. Also go to the night markets and department stores during the change of season sales when you may pick up a bargain or two.

ONE SIZE - TOO SMALL

The Three M's

The above comments about climate and clothes tell you three more things: *Mold*, *Mildew*, and *Moths*! These three M's are the scourge of clothing and a big problem generally in Taiwan. Wallpaper frequently molds or peels off and anything made of leather or fabric which is not regularly used can develop a living ecosystem of its own. The only way to handle this is to use sufficient mothballs in storage and to pack away clothes and blankets at the change of seasons. Pick a dry hot summer day and let the items dry and freshen outside before packing them away. Alternatively, put them in the dryer and iron them immediately before putting them in a box or chest. Dampness forms around floorboards and corners, so be careful to store boxes in dry areas.

TRANSPORT: EXPECT THE WORST

Without question, Taiwan traffic has to be among the worst in the world. It is not just that roads are choked for 20 hours a day with too many cars, motorcycles, and buses, all competing for miniscule advantage. It is not just that there are not enough traffic police and they do not seem to give out tickets for anything but highway speeding. On top of all this, there is the Taiwanese-Confucian sense of responsibility to one's family and to hell with others (which we will explore at more length in Chapter Five). If the traffic rules or right of way do not suit the circumstance of the person driving, they are ignored.

On one occasion, an expat was rear-ended in Taipei traffic. The Taiwanese driver of the offending vehicle insisted that it was the expat's fault; he had stopped too suddenly to avoid another collision. In such circumstances, if the two parties can reach an agreement right there, cash-out-of-pocket, or through an exchange of cards and addresses, then there is no need to call the police. If the police are brought in, the offender must pay a procedural fee. The two could not agree and so the Taiwanese man insisted on calling the police. When the police arrived he rushed over to them and explained he had called them. "Whose car is the one behind?" the cop asked immediately.

"Mine," the Taiwanese said.

"And *you* called us?" the policeman asked incredulously.

Yes, the concept of right of way is legally alive in Taiwan, but it is not too healthy in the minds of drivers. Prepare for the worst and learn to look left, right, up, and down before you cross the street.

Taxis

If you do not have a car, you will immediately begin to rely on taxis (*jichengche*). Taxis are plentiful, metered, and quite reasonably priced. It is very possible that when you alight, the driver will ask you for more than the fare on the meter. He is probably not trying to cheat you. The authorities revise fares periodically and rather than get new meters, they will carry a conversion chart around. If this happens to you, pay the higher fare. During Chinese New Year and when going to distant or difficult places, drivers will sometimes demand negotiated fares.

Thankfully, Taiwan now has radio-alerted taxi fleets. But note that they will add NT$10 to the meter for this service. Unfortunately, we are not aware of any English language phone service for these fleets, so you will either need help to call them or will have to learn to speak Mandarin.

Taxis are known to drive much faster than the traffic allows, causing much concern to the uninitiated passenger. Learn to say, "*Ching, man yi dyan,*" (A little slower, please) to the taxi driver.

For long-haul taxi trips (Taipei to Taichung or Kaohsiung), there are the so-called 'wild chicken taxis' (*yejiche*). It is a name well-earned by these coarse speed demons who will try to get a full complement of four paying passengers to squeeze into their cars for a fast and risky ride. These fellows are reputedly 'hopped up' on stimulants and make as many trips as they can squeeze into the day or night. They wait for prey at the rail, bus, and downtown air terminals. Best to either book long-haul trips with someone known to your company, drive yourself, or take the bus or train.

Automobiles

Owning and operating an automobile in Taiwan is an expensive affair. Although local prices of imported cars have dropped over the past decade as the government liberalized import duties, the New Taiwan Dollar has appreciated, thereby making the foreign currency price (your home price) still high. Expect to pay close to double what the vehicle would cost in the United States, Europe, or Japan.

To legally own and operate a vehicle or obtain a local driver's license, you must have obtained your alien residence certificate. If you do not have this, you can still lease a car. But be sure to have a valid driver's license from your home country before you come. It will allow you to legally drive in Taiwan for the first month of your stay and then you can readily apply for a local license. You can get a local license even if you have no valid international permit, but it is time consuming, involves medical examinations (even the teeth!), and application forms in Mandarin only.

Used vehicles are available. Make sure you get all the proper documentation, which should include a contract of sale, certificate of previous ownership, and vehicle registration papers. The car dealer should be willing to assist you with all the paperwork. Make this a condition of purchase.

Ask the dealer to brief you on the various inspections and taxes you will be expected to pay and when. Also shop around for your insurance and be sure to buy it, preferably maximum coverage. Driving in Taiwan is not a picnic. Accidents do occur, the locals are under-insured, and they appear to go for higher claims when involved in an accident with a foreigner. If you are drawn into a court settlement, the aggrieved can prevent you from departing the country until the claim is settled.

As important as the car itself, is where you will park it. Construction companies have studiously ignored city planning edicts to include sufficient parking in their building projects, so finding a parking space is a true nightmare. Many people will spend as much time in the search for a space every morning as they do in the commute. The alternatives are not much better:

- Buy a space in your office building. This might cost the same amount as the car itself.
- Hire a driver who worries about the parking for you—an even costlier option.
- Queue up to use hourly underground and surface parking decks.
- Comb the streets for an open space in a public parking area. These are either metered or attendant-based. Look for the attendant when you park and pay them. If you leave your vehicle before they get to you they will put a parking ticket on the window. Pay this when you return to your car or face a stiff penalty.
- Try to find a free but questionably legal space in an alley or lane.
- Park it illegally.

You can pay fines for public parking at any of the aluminum parking attendant booths throughout the city. They look similar to some stalls that sell bus tickets and magazines, so learn to differentiate them.

If you parked your car questionably and it disappears, look on the sidewalk for Chinese chalk scribbles of your vehicle number and its new location. Breathe a sigh of relief: your car was not stolen. Recovering it is tedious, but organized. Go to the recovery location with your vehicle registration papers and driver's license. The fine will be NT$1,500 if you recover it immediately. They add NT$200 for each day the vehicle remains in the lot. If you cannot find your car, call 5057631 on a tone phone (which will give you instructions in English), then press the hex button (#) followed by your license plate number. The location of your car will be explained to you (in Mandarin!).

Gasoline is expensive and sold by the liter. Until recently, the government-owned China Petroleum Corporation had a monopoly on legitimate pumping stations (*jyayoujan*). Consequently, their locations are infrequent, poorly marked, and the service only just satisfactory. Top off your tank when it reaches the quarter mark. Do not wait too long and then have to search for a station—you probably won't find one in time.

Getting a smaller but sturdy car will certainly help you to find driving easier in Taiwan's city traffic. If you plan a lot of freeway travel, a stronger, more protective vehicle is advised. However, smaller cars are easier to thread through the eye-of-the-needle openings that confront you and are easier to park in the half spaces sometimes left as the only options.

There is frequently gridlock on Taipei's roads which, coupled with the fight for parking spaces, makes driving in the city far from convenient.

Give yourself plenty of time to get to destinations. Stay cool and try to laugh at the insanity you see around you. There is a method in their madness. An essayist once wrote that there is a *Tao* to the traffic, which flows like water, the molecules of the liquid flowing closely packed, but softly moving around obstacles. Taiwan drivers, just like Nature itself, abhor a vacuum. If there is an empty space in front of you on the road, two cars, a bus, and a motorcycle will be sucking themselves into it. A two-lane road becomes a conduit for three lanes of cars and one sliver of motorcycles. Without such Taoist driving, there would be only gridlock. There are just too many vehicles for the road system.

On the highway, do not expect more road courtesy. The meleé is merely sped up and with higher stakes. Always stay alert when you are driving. Be aware that the north-south freeway is not free at all; it is a toll road. A single toll is NT$40. Prepare change or buy a book of 10 tickets at the tollbooth or post office. Freeway rest stops have been established several of the exits. They sell gasoline, snacks, and have toilets.

Motorcycles

An alternative to owning a car, especially if you are single, have no children, or are on a tight budget, is to buy a motorcycle (*mwotwoche* or *jiche*). Taiwan reportedly has the highest per capita ownership of motorcycles in the world. Any major intersection during the day looks like the starting line of some urban motocross race. When traffic lights are on red, motorcycles will weave their way up through the lines of densely packed cars and deposit themselves right at the front. In the crowd it is not unusual to see a family of five balancing on a Vespa. Junior is standing between Dad's legs, Mom sits behind Dad carrying the baby, and Big Sis is clinging on behind Mom. By the time the light changes, as many as 50 to 100 motorcyclists may be revving their engines as they race off in clouds of blue smoke.

If you are planning to join their ranks, be aware that motorcycles are the second-class citizens of the road in Taiwan. When a slow lane is allocated for turning traffic, motorcycles must use that lane only. In any event, motorcycles are not allowed into the fast left-hand lane. At many intersections, motorcycles are not allowed to turn left because that would necessitate being in the fast lane. In this case, they are required to wait for the green light, go through the intersection (staying to the right), and then pull into a special waiting box sometimes painted on the road in front of the pedestrian crosswalk. Here they will await the light to change again.

The advantages of a motorcycle are:
* relatively no parking problems
* able to move through traffic more easily
* cheaper

The downside is:
* dangerous
* frequently inclement weather
* no hauling capacity for groceries, etc.
* no 'face' (see Chapter Five)

You can legally drive a motorcycle under 50cc if you are over 18 and show your overseas driver's license at the Highway Bureau Office. They will give you a local license. For larger bikes, you will be required to take a road test and a written test, as well as a physical examination.

Many expatriates (especially among those who do not have work permits and alien residence certificates) buy motorcycles. However, they often do not get licensed, do not have insurance, and ride around for years on their iron horses. But be warned that it is illegal and you could be in big trouble if you have an accident. Judge for yourself.

City Buses

There is no single bus service procedure in Taipei. There are both government buses and over a dozen local bus companies. The Mandarin for bus is *gung gung chiche* or *gungche*. Bus routes are differentiated by numbers and stops are marked with signs in different shapes and colors, with destinations and further stops written in Chinese only. Buses are divided into air-conditioned and non-air-conditioned types. Fares are based on the number of sectors traveled in the city and the type of bus. Pay your fare either when you board (if you see the character *shang* 上) or when alighting (when you see *sya* 下), depending on the bus company. On non-air-conditioned buses, the fare for adults is NT$8 per sector and it can be paid in exact change or with a ticket. Tickets can be bought either singly or in a card of 10 from kiosks nearby. The fare for adults on air-con buses is NT$10 per sector, which must be paid in exact change only.

Until you get the hang of the bus system, it is best to ask for help and to have someone write destinations in Chinese for you. People in Taiwan are usually friendly and approachable, and if they are waiting for a bus they will help you to pick out the best one to take. When you see the right bus approaching, flag it down. You can show the destination to the ticket collector and he or she will sometimes help to alert you when it is time to get off. To alight, you must pull the bell cord or push the bell button to tell the driver to stop at the next stop. Be sure not to miss the last bus home (usually between 11:00 and 11:30 p.m.).

Mass Rapid Transit

Taipei will soon be home to Taiwan's first and long overdue urban surface/subway mass transit system. At the time of writing, the system was not operational and was the subject of much political infighting and disputes with contractors because of alleged corruption. However, once completed it will be a more convenient and efficient method of travel for most city dwellers, and it should take some of the traffic off Taipei's overcrowded roads.

Bicycles and Walking

As medium and short distance alternatives, these environment-friendly modes of transport are effective in Taiwan. But exercise maximum caution when traveling this way on the road. You may be moving more slowly than the rest of the traffic, but we urge you to wear a bike helmet..

Navigation

Taipei is a big city and its roads are presently in a shambles while the Mass Rapid Transit system is built. Consequently, many expats have found trying to use local maps a complete nightmare. Fully detailed maps are only in Chinese and the semi-detailed maps (such as the ones found in the free *This Month in Taiwan* guide) are adequate only to orient yourself and to find major roads. With help, you may be able to use them to get to desired destinations. Give yourself lots of time and exercise maximum patience during the first few months when you are venturing out to appointments.

There are two elevated freeways that run north-south through Taipei city. These are called Shinsheng and Jiankuo roads. Both of them have public parking stops built underneath them. Curiously, there are no east-west freeways in the city, making a traverse of the town painfully slow.

Street Names

As part of its socialization program, when the Kuomintang recovered Taiwan from Japan, they rewrote the map of Taipei city. If you know the geography, philosophy, and political history of Mainland China, it will help you with street names. Many major boulevards are named after social and political principles, or famous people: Chungshan Road (after Sun Jung Shan a k a. Sun Yat Sen); Minchuan, Mintsu and Minsheng roads (named after Sun Yat Sen's *Three Principles of the People*); and Renai and Chunghsiao roads (meaning 'benevolence' and 'loyalty to country and family' respectively). North, south, east, and west, Taipei has streets and lanes named after cities or geographical features in China. They also correspond to their relative location in the Mainland. Emei, Chengtu, and Kunming are all in Sichuan Province in the southwest of China and, as streets, are all located in the southwest quadrant of Taipei city.

Addresses

The details of addresses written in Chinese come in declining order of magnitude. They roughly follow this format, although they may not include all the graduations below:

Country

City

District

Road or Street

Road Section Number

Lane or Alley Number

Building Number

Floor Number

Door Number

Company or Person

When translated into English on name cards or advertisements, this is somewhat reversed, but the information often gets jumbled up and confusing punctuation creeps in. For example:

Wholesome Goodies Pte Ltd, Rm. 1025 Shin Shin Bldg., 96, Chungshan N. Rd. Sec. 2, Taipei, Taiwan;

or

Noodle Trading Inc., 20 Floor, No. 26, Lane 76, Tachih St., Sanchung, Taipei, Taiwan 241.

If you are confused, ask friends and colleagues to clarify which numbers refer to the building, street, postal district, etc.

PUBLIC FACILITIES AND ASSOCIATIONS

Because Taiwanese culture and language have represented such a barrier to Westerners in the past, an extensive variety of clubs and associations have sprung up which cater to the needs of the expatriate. There are clubs for everything from bridge to bungee jumping. There is the American Club, the Correspondents' Club, the Bankers' Club, the Australian/New Zealanders' Social Group, and many more which you can find out about through the larger expatriate clubs and associations.

Welcoming Services

There are several organizations in Taipei that are devoted to helping English-speaking expatriates settle in. They can be invaluable in helping to ease your family into its new lifestyle.

- **The Community Services Center** is the compiler of the indispensable *Taipei Living* guidebook (see Bibliography), in which you will find complete details and addresses for all the public facilities, clubs, associations and schools in Taiwan. The Center is a non-profit- making organization located in Tienmu and is open on weekdays during normal business hours. They offer Newcomer Orientation Programs—very helpful in getting settled in. Even after you have read this book, remember the Chinese

65

saying, "A thousand words are never as good as a look." Having someone to personally introduce you to Taiwan *in situ* is so much more helpful. The Center also offers cross-cultural training, various classes, professional counseling and organized hikes and tours. Their address, phone, and fax number can be found in the Bibliography.

* **Gateway** is affiliated to the Taipei International Church, but offers non-denominational help to arriving families who are trying to overcome the stress of the move. They maintain a library of information helpful in getting settled in and their staff are available to answer your questions on weekdays from 8:30 a.m. to 4:00 p.m. A welcoming coffee morning is held each Wednesday at 10:00 a.m. Their address is:

   Gateway,
   4F, 438 Chungshan North Road, Sec. 6,
   Tienmu
   Tel: 8719031

* **Our Place** is a support group for expatriate women, open weekday afternoons. It sponsors a lending library and runs special activities:

   Our Place,
   3F, Room 304,
   770 Chungshan North Road, Sec. 6,
   Tienmu
   Tel: 8712614

Libraries and Translation Services

A limited number of private and public lending libraries with extensive English language resource materials do exist in Taiwan. In addition, several companies offer translation services for written documents or conversations, which may be of use to you at some time. However, these services tend to be expensive. In the long run, it is better to try to learn the language or employ staff who can cope in a bilingual environment.

Schools

There are a growing number of international schools which have been set up by various nationalities within the expatriate community and missionary organizations. Depending on the ebb and flow of expatriate transfers, obtaining tuition at the school of your choice can be problematic. Contact the school prior to accepting your assignment in Taiwan to ensure that a space will be available for your children. Enrolling your child in a school that has a curriculum similar to your home school will help to ease the culture shock the child might experience.

HELPING YOUR FAMILY STAY SANE

What causes culture shock? It is basically an accumulation of stress caused by a lack of the familiar. Familiar cues received from the environment (for example, telephones that ring a certain way, signs that communicate in a certain way, toilets that look, feel or flush a certain way) are suddenly gone. Familiar cues received from people in our own culture are also gone, and familiar stress-relievers (like a talk with your mother, your favorite soap opera, even your favorite brand of aspirin) may be absent.

Culture shock can hit the young, the old, the experienced, the naive. It can hit early or late during a tour overseas. It might only be a fleeting moment of melancholy, or a brief loneliness, but it can also be a profound and deep depression.

Understanding what it is can help us to prepare for its onslaught and we can immunize ourselves by slowly immersing into the host culture. Just as one can get used to a hot or cold bath by slowly easing into the water and not shocking the system, so one can slowly ease into the new culture.

We have advised that, given the opportunity, you should take a house-hunting trip to Taiwan. This initial visit as a half-tourist, half-house-hunter, will give you a much better idea of what to expect. You will have a chance to return right away, sharing your adventures and concerns with friends and relatives, and feeling their support and sympathy. This is not to say that a tour of duty in Taiwan is a death sentence, but there are sacrifices to be made. You will not fully appreciate the rewards until you have spent some time in the country.

Talk with each member of your family about the move well in advance of the departure. Perhaps assign different family members to do a book report or some research on different aspects of the culture, history, or customs of Taiwan. They can then present the report to the family. You could rent Chinese video tapes, eat Chinese food, get some copies of the English language daily papers from Taiwan so they all can read about what is going on.

The next step for immunization is to allow yourself to bring some familiar items with you when you move. These need not be irreplaceable family heirlooms or have a high value. More often than not, they will be mundane things: a blanket with a familiar smell, the well-seasoned cast iron skillet you have used for years, your favorite author's books. Just as Superman has his 'Fortress of Solitude' with familiar things from his home planet, so you should make your home a 'familiarity retreat'.

Re-create familiar routines as much as possible. If the family ate together at 6:30 p.m. before, try to maintain that in the beginning. Be patient and listen to your children and spouse, but lend a strong guiding hand. Maintain communication with your relatives back home and encourage your children to write to grandma and grandpa.

The next step is to acknowledge that there will be stress and stress symptoms. Everything will be changing for all of you. The air you breathe, the water you drink, the food you eat, the way you get around, the people you see, and everything you hear outside will all be new and different. Symptoms of stress can include withdrawal, changes in eating habits, aggression, absent-mindedness, regression of habits (toilet training, bed wetting), etc. Take the time to talk through these manifestations with family members.

Indeed, the most familiar and warm thing you can bring with you from the old home is, and should be, your intrafamilial relationship.

Strengthen it. Spend more time with your children and spouse, not less. The temptation is to dive into work. Set aside time for your family until you can see they are well settled. Try to get them into regular activities of interest to them, such as scouting, gymnastics, bridge.

Finally, share your feelings of shock and loneliness with each other. Let them know that you are feeling the same things that they are, and that you understand and care about their feelings too.

Other expatriates have commented to us that culture shock Taiwanese-style falls heavily on the spouse of the working parent, usually the wife. She may have worked in her native country and had to abandon a job. Her children fit quickly, albeit with varying degrees of stress, into the routine of school. Her husband is out trying to succeed at the business that sent them to Taiwan. That leaves her alone and a stranger. Both partners need to be aware of this and work together to try to make the transition less stressful.

Having prepared yourself for the gradual immersion into the local culture, you can now consciously plan how to get out into it. Take the time to tour some scenic areas with the family. Take long walks together through your neighborhood and environs, and stop and initiate conversations with people. Get out to some of the expatriate meeting areas and meet new people. There are several community centers and aid organizations just for the expatriate community. Contact the several newcomer services that exist. Enroll in language classes and paste up vocabulary stickers in Mandarin all around the house, where they can be in constant sight and make learning easier and more fun.

Soon the strange will become the familiar and angst will become appreciation.

Chapter Four

LANGUAGE

"It rained almost all of yesterday. I went out in the morning to meet the *ganma* (adopted mother I was staying with), Mrs. Chang. She helped me buy an umbrella (*yusan*), a humorous event to recall but embarrassing to live through. We went to one store and looked at an automatic umbrella which cost NT$110. After trying to bargain the man down, unsuccessfully, I said to Mrs. Chang, "*Yesyu women yingdang dau byede pudz chyu.*" (Perhaps we should go to another store.) The quizzical, uncomprehending look on their faces was

noticeable. "Shop down street sell notebooks," she said in halting English. Notebooks?! Apparently I had said *budz* rather than *pudz* and, at any rate, in Taiwan they don't call a store *pudz*, but *syaudyan* or *dyan*. We went to another store and bought the umbrella for NT$100."
—Chris's Diary, July 7, 1976, five days after arriving in Taiwan.

Among the biggest decisions a resident in Taiwan has to face is whether or not to attempt to learn to speak, read, or write Chinese. It is, of course, possible to live as an expatriate professional or resident in Taiwan for many years without developing any proficiency beyond the most rudimentary. I know many men and women who have done so. They are, however, tethered to the American Club or other foreign support activities and organizations, as well as their chauffeurs and maids. To them, the single most difficult barrier to their enjoyment of Taiwan is communication. "Even the telephone operator does not speak English," they would complain.

The decision to learn the language should not be taken lightly, but it will reap rewards for you in terms of your cultural understanding, the depth of friendships you can develop, and the ease with which you can move through otherwise complex and frustrating situations. Whichever you decide, the basic knowledge of the language's relation to the people, explained below, is a must.

The Kuomintang would have one believe that the population of Taiwan is linguistically monolithic, a population of Mandarin speakers. This is not the case. How could it be on an island that was colonized by Hokkien provincials, ceded to the Japanese in the Treaty of Shimonoseki in 1895, and only returned to Chinese rule in 1945? Language, though, became an important tool in the battle to indoctrinate the local population after 1945. It was forbidden under martial law to teach Hokkien in schools and Hokkien language television programming was severely limited. The ruling party felt it imperative to linguistically tie Taiwan to Mainland China.

71

The flip side of this was an emphasis on traditionally written characters (*fantidz*) versus the simplified character syllabary (*jiantidz*) developed by the Communist educators in Mainland China. The use of simplified characters was treated as just another part of the rape of Chinese culture under Communist rule and teachers, students, publishers, and advertisers were forbidden to use them. Somewhere along the way, though, a concession was made. Officials allowed the use of the simplified form of certain characters, such as *tai* (as in Taiwan) with its five strokes rather than the *fanti* form with its 14 strokes. The distinction between written and spoken languages here is culturally important. A major source of Chinese cultural pride is that they feel unique in the world due to a cultural heritage that has lasted continuously for over 4,000 years. The ancient Egyptian civilization did not succeed in continuing. Neither did those of Rome, Greece, Turkey, and Persia. But in China there was no Dark Age, no rise and fall, no sinking into oblivion. What links all Chinese together through this long history is the written language. Each province has its own dialect, and within a province there can be major variations, rendering spoken communication impossible. But, by and large, the written language transcends all the provinces of the Han Chinese.

To understand this better, think of European Romance languages and history. French, Italian, and Spanish all derive from Latin. All utilize the same alphabet to spell their words, but in neither the spoken nor the written language can one be sure of what is being communicated by someone in the other language, unless one knows that language. One can guess at meanings because of similar roots, but that is all. The spoken dialects of Chinese have just as much variance in pronunciation as the Romance languages, but the written language is a common denominator. We will discuss the written language in more detail below, but first a review of what you will be hearing.

MANDARIN

Mandarin is known in Taiwan as *gwoyu* (national language), signaling the political significance the Kuomintang attached to linguistic unity in China. I was told in Beijing that the word 'Mandarin' comes from *Mandaren* (Great Manchu) because during the Manchu Qing Dynasty this language was the *gwan hwa* (language of the government officials). As spoken in Taiwan, it is no longer pure Beijing *hwa* (patois) with its heavy rolling 'R' addends, but a softened, middle-of-the-road language. Vocabulary notwithstanding, pronunciations vary little from the *putong hwa* (common language) taught in Mainland China now and adopted by Singapore as one of its national languages. Because it can be used in these countries and many other places where Chinese people have settled, Mandarin is a valuable asset.

Tones

Mandarin is a tonal language. This means that each word has a pronunciation which carries a tone. Changing the tone changes the meaning. There are four tones and a clear (unstressed) tone:

#1 tone (*yi sheng*)	—	High and even tone
#2 tone (*er sheng*)	╱	Rising tone
#3 tone (*san sheng*)	∨	Dipping tone
#4 tone (*sz sheng*)	╲	Falling tone
(*ching sheng*)	O	Clear tone

A favorite example used to demonstrate tones is the sentence, *Ma-ma ma ma ma*? (Is mama scolding the horse?)

Grammar

Mandarin grammar is relatively simple. To turn a statement into a question, add *ma* to the end. To put it in the past tense, add *le* after the verb or at the end of the sentence. To put it in the future tense, add *yau* or *hwei* (want, will or can) before the verb. To negate it, add *bu* (present) or *mei* (past) before the verb. For example:

Ni chyu Syang Gang.	You go to Hong Kong.
Ni chyu Syang Gang ma?	Are you going (now) to Hong Kong?
Ni chyu le Syang Gang.	You went to Hong Kong
Ni yau chyu Syang Gang.	You will go to Hong Kong.
Ni bu chyu Syang Gang.	You are not going to Hong Kong.
Ni mei chyu Syang Gang.	You did not go to Hong Kong.

This is, of course, grossly over-simplified and tuition in Chinese is best left to a language book and tutor. In this section, though, you will find a primer which may help you get through the first weeks.

TAIWANESE

Taiwanese is the mother tongue spoken outside of school by the majority of the population, who also maintain fluency in Mandarin and use it interchangeably. It is known in Taiwan by several names:

Mandarin	*Meaning*	*Taiwanese Pronunciation*
Taiyu	Taiwan language	*Taigu*
Fujian Hwa	Spoken Fujian	*Hokkien Wei*
Minnan Hwa	Spoken south of the Min River	*Minnan Wei*

As can be understood from the above, Taiwanese was a dialect brought to Taiwan by immigrants who left the area south of the Min River in the Province of Fujian. This distinguishes it from *Fujou* or *Syamen hwa* which are spoken in other areas of the Province of Fujyan.

It is a tonally rich and complex tongue that rises and falls, lending itself to the passionate oratory of the street hawker or opposition politician. One factor that makes its study daunting is its six change-able tones. Mandarin's four tones only change in closely circum-scribed ways. In Taiwanese, a tone may change whether it is at the beginning, the middle, or the end of a sentence. It makes the memo-rization of tones all the more difficult. To make matters more complicated, Taiwanese as spoken in Taipei, Tainan, and Kaohsiung has variations, though communication between these dialect groups is not difficult.

Several Mandarin/Taiwanese comparisons will let you see how different they are:

Mandarin:	*Ni hau ma? Wo shr Meigwo ren.*
Taiwanese:	*Li ho bwo? Ngoa shi Bigok lang.*
English:	How are you? I am an American.

WHAT TO LEARN?

With the choice of Mandarin or Taiwanese, what is one to learn? Ability to converse in Taiwanese will endear you to the Taiwanese population and leave the Mandarin speakers confused or resentful. Fluency in Mandarin, on the other hand, will impress almost everyone; can be used throughout China; and will generally be easier to learn. There are many more texts, tapes, tutors, and schools of Mandarin than Taiwanese, thus increasing your options when learning Mandarin. Unless you are going to be a missionary or a doctor working in remote areas, it is probably best to learn Mandarin first and pick up Taiwanese as and when friends teach it to you. It is important to know that the two languages exist side by side, but you should not let yourself be confused by the fact.

WAYS TO LEARN

Short intensive courses exist for rapidly teaching a foreigner the basics. This is highly recommended if you want to hit the ground running. Keep up the momentum, though. Enroll in a tutorial of several hours per week and use your Mandarin at all available opportunities.

There are four basic ways to learn the language, with or without a teacher:
1. By ear, in which case you try to imitate what you hear and do not commit to writing the sounds.
2. Using romanized text.

3. Using text with the Chinese phonetic alphabet.
4. Using text with Chinese characters only.

The first option is inefficient and will result in many mispronounced words, unless you are truly gifted. Option four is for masochists or people with an unbelievably large amount of free time on their hands. That leaves options two and three.

Romanization

There are many famous and several obscure methods of romanizing the Chinese language (i.e. writing the Chinese sounds in the Roman alphabet). But is there a standard, you ask? Sorry. In Taiwan you will see Chinese romanized in many ways. The Mainland Chinese have instituted the *Pinyin* standard, which has as many deficiencies as any system around and is not accepted by the Kuomintang government in Taiwan. The system the KMT advocate is hardly used at all.

A drawback in using the romanized text to learn to pronounce is that you bring whatever linguistic baggage your own mother tongue carries: accents, pronunciation standards, etc. For instance, there is no way a Frenchman, Mexican, Bostonian, and Singaporean will all pronounce the romanized character *hsueh* in the same way, yet there is only one correct sound. Throughout this text I have used the Yale system because I feel it most closely approximates Chinese sounds. It is not terribly common in textbooks, however.

The Phonetic Alphabet

Besides romanization, one can learn using the Mandarin phonetic symbols. This is an 'alphabet' of 37 symbols which, when combined, can represent all the sounds in Mandarin. Taiwanese kindergarteners and primary schoolchildren learn this way. In addition, the *Gwoyu Ri Bau*, a local daily newspaper, shows the symbols next to all the characters in the text of the paper. By learning the way children do, from fundamental phonetic building blocks, you are much more likely to be able to pronounce correctly. Unfortunately, it is only at the

Gwoyu Ri Bau language classes where you will definitely use these symbols. Check with the individual school you enroll at to see if they use them, but note that the Mandarin phonetic symbols are not seen outside of Taiwan.

A comparison of the phonetic symbols of the different romanization systems is given below. As you can see, the difference in spelling suggests a vastly different pronunciation for what should be the same sounds.

Yale	Pinyin	Wade-Giles	Kwoyeu	Chinese
bwo	bo	po	bor	ㄅ
pwo	po	p'o	po	ㄆ
mwo	mo	mo	mo	ㄇ
fwo	fo	fo	for	ㄈ
de	de	te	dih	ㄉ
te	te	t'e	teh	ㄊ
ne	ne	ne	ne	ㄋ
le	le	le	le	ㄌ
ge	ge	ke	geh	ㄍ
ke	ke	k'e	keh	ㄎ
he	he	he	her	ㄏ
ji	ji	chi	jyi	ㄐ
chi	qi	ch'i	chi	ㄑ
syi	xi	hsi	shyi	ㄒ
jr	zhi	chih	jyy	ㄓ
chr	chi	ch'ih	chyy	ㄔ
shr	shi	shih	shyr	ㄕ
r	ri	jih	ryh	ㄖ
dz	zi	tzu	tzy	ㄗ
ts	c	ts'	tsy	ㄘ

sz	s	sz, ss	sy	
a	a	a	a	ㄚ
o	o	o	o	ㄛ
e	e	e	e	ㄜ
e	e	e	e	ㄝ
ai	ai	ai	ai	ㄞ
ei	ei	ei	ei	ㄟ
au	ao	ao	au	ㄠ
ou	ou	ou	ou	ㄡ
an	an	an	an	ㄢ
en	en	en	en	ㄣ
ang	ang	ang	ang	ㄤ
eng	eng	eng	eng	ㄥ
er	r	erh	el	ㄦ
yi	i	i	i	一
u	u	u	u	ㄨ
yu	u	ui	u	ㄩ

MANDARIN PRIMER
People

I *Wo*

We/Us *Women*

Mr. *Syansheng*

Person *Ren*

You *Ni*

You *Nimen*

Mrs. *Taitai*

Possessive particle *De*

Him/Her *Ta*

They/Them *Tamen*

Miss *Syauye*

Courtesies

Please *Ching*

Excuse me *Dweibuchi*

May I ask? *Ching wen?*

Good evening *Wan an*

Thank you *Syesye*

How are you? *Ni hau ma?*

Good morning *Dzau an*

Goodbye *Dzai jyan*

Basic Verbs

To go *Chyu*	To want *Yau*	To come *Lai*
To walk *Dzou*	To eat *Chr*	To read/See *Kan*
To sit *Dzwo*	To buy *Mai*	To write *Sye*
To say *Shwo*	To hear *Ting*	To think *Syang*
To open *Kai*	To close *Guan*	To live (in) *Ju*
To be *Shr*	To be able *Hwei*	To be good *Hau*
To use *Yung*	To have *You*	To tell *Gausu*
To know *Jrdau*		
Question word *Ma?*	Verb negater *Bu/Mei*	Past tense *Le*

Directional

To/Towards *Dau*	Down *Sya*	Up *Shang*
Inside *Limyan*	Outside *Waimyan*	From *Tsung*
At *Dzai*	This *Jeige*	That *Neige*
Here *Jeili*	There *Nali*	

Places

Airport *Jichang*	Hotel *Dafandyan*	School *Sywesyau*
Restaurant *Tsanting*	Hospital *Yiyuan*	Home *Jyali*
Cinema *Dyanying yuan*	Toilet *Tseswo*	Bar *Jyouba*
Kitchen *Chufang*	Living room *Keting*	Bedroom *Wofang*
America *Meigwo*	Australia *Aujou*	Indonesia *Yinni*
Ticket window *Shoupyauchu*	Department store *Baihwogungsz*	

Things

Automobile *Chiche*	Airplane *Feiji*	Taxi *Jichengche*
Telephone *Dianhwa*	Television *Dyanshr*	Door *Men*
Suitcase *Syinglisyang*	Chair *Yidz*	Book *Shu*
Key *Yaushr*	Chopsticks *Kwaidz*	Bowl *Wan*
Glass *Beidz*	Coca-cola *Kekoukele*	Beer *Pijyou*
Table *Jwodz*	Steamed rice *Baifan*	Water *Shwei*

Mandarin *Gwoyu*
Chinese food *Junggwo fan*
Vegetable market *Tsai shr chang*

English *Yingyu*
Western food *Syit san*

Time

Today *Jintyan*
Hour *Syaushr*
Day *Tyan*

Yesterday *Dzwotyan* Tomorrow *Mingtyan*
Minute *Fenjung*   Month *Yue*
Day after tomorrow *Houtyan*

Numbers

One *Yi*
Four *Sz*
Seven *Chi*
Ten *Shr*
Hundred *Bai*
Thousand *Chyan*
Money *Chyan*
Expensive *Gwei*

Two *Er*
Five *Wu*
Eight *Ba*
Sixteen *Shrlyou*
Three hundred *Sanbai*
Seven thousand *Chichyan*
Dollars *Kwaichyan*
Cheap *Pyanyi*

Three *San*
Six *Lyou*
Nine *Jyou*
Twenty *Ershr*

Question Words

What? *Shemma?*   Why *Weishemma?*   How? *Dzemma?*
When? *Shemma shrhou?*   Why *Weishemma?*
How much *Dwoshau?*   Where? *Nali?*

Forming Phrases

The words above can create countless combinations of logical and useful sentences, as shown below. Read the Chinese romanizations and the translations, then look up the words to see and understand how the sentence is constructed. Practice constructing your own sentences. As noted before, Chinese grammar is the easiest part of the task at hand.

Wo tsung Meigwo lai. Wo ju dzai dafandyan.
I came from America. I live in a hotel.

Chen Syansheng shr Taiwan ren. Ta hwei shwo Yingyu.
Mr. Chen is Taiwanese. He can speak English.

Jintyan, Wo syang chr Junggwo fan, Wo bu yau chr Syi tsan. Hau bu hau?
Today, I am thinking of eating Chinese food, I do not want Western food. Okay?

Mingtyan, Ta yau dzwo jichengche dau jichang chyu. Ta yau yung dwoshau chyan?
Tomorrow, he wants to ride (sit) in a taxi to go to the airport. How much money will he need (use)?

Wo jude dafandyan gwei. Yi tyan wu chyan kwaichyan. Ching gausu Wo, you mei you pyanyi de?
The hotel I live in is expensive. One day (costs) five thousand dollars. Please tell me, are there (have or not have) cheaper (ones)?

Dzwo chiche dau Taijung yau san ge syaushr. Ni yau chyu ma?
It takes three hours to drive to Taichung. Do you want to go?

Weishemma bu yau mai jwodz? Tai gwei ma? Dwoshau chyan?
Why don't (you) want to buy the table? Is it too expensive? How much money?

Syesye ni gausu wo dzemma dzou dau tsanting chyu.
Thank you for telling me how to get (walk) to the restaurant.

Chingwen, yiyuan dzai nali?
Please, where is a hospital?

Follow the Bouncing Ball

Once the basic language is picked up, one of the best and quickest ways Chris has found to increase vocabulary and fluency is to learn popular songs. You will hear them playing on the radio and eventually you will catch one that appeals to you. Go out and buy the cassette, which invariably includes the lyrics, sit down with your dictionary, look up all the new words, understand and learn the song. It is like solving a mystery. Here is a melody you like and you can hear the emotion of the singer, but you have no idea what they're singing about. As you translate, the story unfolds. The best thing is that once the song is learned, you can sing it to yourself and review the vocabulary that way; it's much easier to remember. You can draw vocabulary, sophisticated and fresh, from the song to use in conversation. Knowing local pop songs will also help to break the ice at a karaoke session!

Poetry

China has a long and wonderful tradition of poetry. The poetry of the Tang Dynasty (A.D. 618–907) is a major part of elementary school language studies and pupils must learn to recite the most famous verses. Many of the most famous poems are short and are easily accessible to the foreign student of Mandarin. They will at once give you a deeper understanding of Chinese culture and the universal kinship of man.

Idioms

The Chinese have a long history of pithy expressions. The original writings of Lau Tzu, Confucius, and others were all very spare and obscure. This is why translations vary so widely in quality and content. The translator is trying to express in English, for example, what was said with only four or five characters and finds he needs a dozen or two words to do it justice. From the classics and historical stories come many phrases—four character expressions called *cheng yu*. There are literally tens of thousands of these which Chinese sprinkle into their conversation from time to time. They defy definition with an equal number of English words. Some examples:

- *Saiweng shr ma* (old Sai looses his horse) derives from the story of a man who, beset with hardship and misfortune, claims equanimity to his friends who lament his difficulties. In the end his judgement is shown to be correct. The saying is used to express a lack of concern when things do not go right.

- *Dz syang mau dwun* (mutually facing shield and spear) derives from the story of a hawker who is laughed out of town when he tries to simultaneously sell a spear that can penetrate anything and a shield that is impenetrable. This is used to point out basic contradictions in an argument.

Idioms are good to learn from a cultural point of view, can give you a beginner's taste for the traditional language, and can help you to understand other people's conversation. However, they should be used with caution unless one is very sure of the context. They are easily abused. It would be like an American scattering his conversation with Shakespearean quotations on a visit to England.

Jokes

If the television and movie comedies are any indication, the Taiwanese enjoy puerile, slapstick humor—flatulence and food fights. Taiwan has a long history of stand-up comedy and comic dialogues, but, unlike other cultures with other languages, there does not seem to be a widespread cult of joke-telling amongst the Chinese. Normally, if friends gather together, they might tell humorous tales about themselves, with some exaggeration thrown in to pump up the laughs. They usually would not recite a repertoire of jokes as Westerners do. Self-deprecating humor is well-accepted. Popular comedians tend to be exaggerations themselves; porky, skinny, memorable in a crazy way. You certainly do not hear jokes about politicians and current events, the way Western comedians like Jay Leno or the BBC's *Two Cheers for the Month of ...* would do. Books are sold about Chinese humor, but we have not heard many jokes told. The Taiwanese prefer to laugh at themselves.

If you wish to tell jokes, you must be careful. English language jokes will fall flat unless your audience is fluent in the language. If you translate foreign humor into Chinese, it will only travel well providing the jokes are not dependent on word play for their meaning and the words create a mental picture that provides the humor. Jokes in which a physical action bolster the mental image are good.

For example, a Chinese joke that translates well goes like this: 'Three teetotallers walk past a wine house. One man says, "I can't tolerate alcohol. One glass of beer, my face turns red, and I stumble about until I pass out."

The next man says, "That's nothing. If I even smell a glass of beer, I turn red and want to pass out, drunk."

Then the third man pipes up, "You think you two have a problem. If I even look at someone who has smelled beer, I get drunk!" '

On the other hand, an example of a Western joke that translates well is this one:

'A farmer is plowing the fields with his ox, when suddenly the ox stops pulling, sits down, turns round to the farmer and says, "It's too goddamn hot. I won't pull another foot." The farmer is stunned and begins a conversation with the animal. His neighbor is walking with his dog down the road and sees the ox taking its leisure. He decides to take a closer look. When he asks the farmer what gives, the ox replies, "It's too goddamn hot. I won't pull another foot." The neighbor is so frightened he picks up his dog and makes a run for it. When he tires out, he settles under the shade of a tree and ponders aloud what he has witnessed, "Gracious, that's the first time I have ever seen a talking ox!"

"Me too!" the dog replies.'

Among mixed, gentle company, jokes with a sexual overtone should be avoided, though the hostesses at drinking establishments can probably tell five saucy jokes to your every one and would feign enjoy hearing yours. Among members of the same gender, judge for yourself whether the mood and place are right for such humor.

Swearing

The Taiwanese do swear and the most frequent epithet you will hear is *ta ma de*! which literally means 'his mother's'. His mother's what? We are left to suppose. Some rough people will begin or end practically every sentence with this.

Insults tend to be of the dehumanizing variety, such as calling a person a dog. The Taiwanese will not understand the intention of most four-letter words in English, but it does not mean you should use them or translate them with impunity. Your angry intentions may well be understood on a visceral level and you might find you have a fight on your hands. Taiwanese are emotional and the wrong people in the wrong place can have a short fuse.

BODY LANGUAGE

The Chinese have a reputation for being inscrutable, but this does not really stem from body language. Many of the body language cues that would tip you off in a Western encounter will be valid in Taiwan: arms folded across the chest ('I do not agree'), yawning ('you are a bore'), stomach rumbling ('let's eat').

What you will find difficult is that much is left unsaid. When two Taiwanese enter into a conversation, they usually have a strong understanding of their own interrelationship and the rules of that relationship. So, to speak of certain things would be considered rudely abrupt or superfluous. However, you as a Westerner will enter the conversation not only ignorant of the rules, but also of your relationship with them. You might be treating the person condescendingly when they perceives their position as superior to yours, or vice versa.

The American penchant to treat everyone equally can be misconstrued here. A third person who sees you treat their junior the same way as you treated them will not understand your cultural background and may begin twisting in theri mind why you have acted that way. You will also frequently come out of conversations without a clear idea of what has been agreed upon in the other person's mind. Learn to graciously act in the superior role when it is appropriate.

Because there is a multitude of possible scenarios, we cannot here go into specific detail about how to act. We suggest you read Chapter Six very carefully to learn more about the unwritten rules in relating to the Taiwanese. In general, remember that it is relative standing that dictates what is proper for a person to say and how she or he treats the other person.

Depending on the culture you come from, you may find Taiwanese personal distance uncomfortable. The Taiwanese do not mind sitting close to someone and if you are a friend (man to man, or woman to woman) they might occasionally touch your hand or take your arm. Do not be alarmed; this is not a homosexual advance, just a gesture from a person who is comfortable enough with you to get that close. It means that you are making progress. Among students or old folk, you will frequently notice members of the same sex walking arm in arm, or sometimes holding hands. This is not abnormal; the contact is gentle and subtle. However, they do not like loud, back-slapping, bear-hugging, cheek-kissing contact of the sort at which some Americans and Europeans excel. Similarly, physical contact with strangers of the opposite sex is limited to handshakes. At what point this person is no longer a stranger and you can feel free to touch them varies according to the individual.

Like other cultures, the Taiwanese sometimes use hand gestures as a form of communication. It is useful to briefly go over these, so that you can understand more about unwritten communication and minimize embarrassing mistakes.

- To encourage a person to move toward you, extend the arm out, palm down, and wave your fingers toward yourself.
- To point to yourself, use your index finger and point at your nose.
- When someone touches their index finger to their cheek and scratches it up and down (especially when saying *"Chyou chyou lian"*) they are indicating that a person has 'lost face'.
- To hold the fist up and draw the index finger two or three times, like pulling a trigger, means that someone or something is dead or finished.
- Taiwanese do not use or understand the 'middle finger'. If you angrily shake your fist at someone, though, you will get the deserved response.
- Showing numbers on fingers varies from the West. One through five are initiated with the thumb, but the Chinese have developed special signs for six, eight, and 10.

Six: hold your fist up, palm up, with the thumb and pinky extended. Eight: hold your fist down, palm down, with the thumb and pinky extended (looks like the character for eight).Ten: create a cross with your left and right index fingers (looks like the character for 10).

THE WRITTEN WORD

Definitely the hardest part of mastering the Chinese language is the written characters. Over 50,000 in number, there is no end to learning them. The characters evolved from deep in China's past, from drawings of elements of life essential to the Chinese. Over thousands of years, these rough drawings were stylized, simplified, modified, and codified to become the written word of today. Even now, Chinese characters remain pictographs. One can still see the elements from which they are derived:

羊 (*yang*) ram, see the horns.

川 (*chwan*) stream, see the flowing water.

山 (*shan*) mountain, see the peak.

Characters are usually made up of two components: the radical and the phonetic complement. One should first become familiar with all the radicals (numbering 214) and their original meanings. Radicals will frequently give a clue to the meaning, or at least the category of the word.

For example, 酉 (*you*) is defined by the dictionary as being the tenth of the Twelve Terrestrial Branches and as the period on the traditional Chinese clock corresponding to 5:00–7:00 p.m. Most characters using this radical, though, are associated with wine, drunkenness, and fermentation. The wisdom of the ancients—they understood the concept of the 'happy hour' so well!

Phonetic complements are written above, below or beside the radical and help give a clue to the pronunciation.

酉 (*you*) + 卒 (*swei*) = 醉 *dzwei* (to be drunk)

酉 (*you*) + 星 (*sying*) = 醒 *sying* (to recover from drunkenness)

酉 (*you*) + 余 (*yu*) = 酴 *tu* (brewer's yeast)

Other examples of radical/phonetic complement couplings are:

氵 (*shwei*) water + 羊 (*yang*) = 洋 *yang* (ocean)

食 (*shr*) comestibles + 反 (*fan*) = 飯 *fan* (rice)

金 (*jin*) gold + 戔 (*jyan*) = 錢 *chyan* (money)

Stroke Order

Remembering the words is not enough. To claim knowledge of the written language, one must be able to remember the proper stroke order in writing characters. A Westerner fresh off the boat can find any number of ways to complete the image of the character, but there is, alas, only one correct way, and your Chinese friends will not let you forget it if they see you err. There are many practice books prepared for first graders that take a 'paint by numbers' approach and guide you through the proper order. If you want to learn to write, start here. After learning several hundred characters, the stroke order of others will come naturally.

Calligraphy

Still, you have not reached the pinnacle of achievement. To do so, you must now take brush in hand and learn traditional calligraphy. This is an art, a way of life, and a form of personal expression. In other words it can be esoteric and subjective in the extreme, consuming a brief moment of your time or your entire life. It is considered to be meditative, and superior calligraphy is the highest expression of a cultured person's demeanor.

NAMES

Chinese names can be confusing to the Westerner as they are written in the reverse order of English names. The surname or family name (*sying*) appears first, while the given name (*ming*) comes last. For this reason, it is inappropriate to ask questions like, "What is your last name?" or "What is your Christian name?" Better to ask, "What is your surname/given name?"

There are several hundred surnames in Chinese. Some of the most popular are: Lee (a. k. a. Li), Chen (a. k. a. Tan), Wu, Lin (a. k. a. Lim), Ma, Wang, Hwang (a. k. a. Huang), Guo (a. k. a. Kuo), Tsai (a. k. a. T'sai) and Su. However, when romanized on a name card, it is difficult to know whether the person has changed the *sying/ming* order to accommodate Westerners, or left it in the original order. Sometimes punctuation can give a clue. Consider, for example, the name Lee Guo Tsai. Each of these words is a potential surname. Is he Mr. Lee or Mr. Tsai? 'Lee Guo-tsai' or 'Lee, Guo Tsai' tells you his surname is Lee. Many Taiwanese will forego romanizing their given names and simply put 'G. T. Lee' for example, thereby making things a lot easier for you.

However, some Taiwanese business people have added a Western given name to their cards. While most of these are simple off-the-shelf names, like Robert or Simon, others are more obscure, like Jubilee, Beauty, or Banjo. Get into the habit of underlining the surname of business contacts on their name cards when you meet them. To make matters more confusing, there do exist several Chinese surnames which are two characters. They are rare but you should be aware of them. Sz Tu is an example. More common, but still unusual, are single-character given names.

Names are important to the Taiwanese. They denote one's family lineage and can refer to one's status within that family. For instance the title *Syansheng* (Mr.) literally means 'first born' and shows the importance placed within the family on the number-one son. Similarly, *Taitai* means 'wife' or 'Mrs.', but literally translated means 'ultimate, ultimate'—the number-one wife, as opposed to the lesser-standing concubines and mistresses of tradition. *Syaujye*, on the other hand, means 'Miss' or, literally, 'little big sister'.

Much time is spent in naming children according to their date of birth, zodiac sign, and the propitious number of strokes to be included in the characters which make up the whole name. The Taiwanese want the name to be as lucky and auspicious as possible. Note also that, in many families, the first character of the given name (or miuddle name) indicates the generation of the person within the family tree. In other words, all members born in that generation of that family line will have the same character in their names. For example, Wu Ling-li's sisters are Ling-yu, Ling-mei, and Ling-lan.

Armed with this knowledge, several productive and endearing minutes can be spent with Taiwanese friends, fully understanding the significance of their names.

How to Address the Taiwanese

How you address your Taiwanese friends and contacts will, of course, depend on their relation to you (business or personal), and whether you are speaking English or Mandarin. Let's assume you are learning to speak the language. If this is your first business contact with a particular person, it is best to address him or her with their surname followed by the title on the name card. For instance, you should call Lee Chang Jang, 'Factory Manager Lee', or Chen Dzung Jing Li, 'General Manager Chen Dzung', if these are their job designations. This gives proper attention to their title (of which they should be proud) and helps you to avoid the problem of how to address a businesswoman of whose marital status you are unsure.

If you are speaking English, it is best to stick with Mr., Mrs., Madame, or Miss, plus the person's surname. When you become better friends, he or she may ask you to use their adopted English name. Even among close Taiwanese friends, it is not common to use the given name. Nicknames are more common. Adding the term *lau* (old) to the surname of elders is quite common, e.g. Lau Lee, or Lau Chen. However, a person will tell you when you can address them as such. Assume nothing!

Adopting a Chinese Name

In Japan, Westerners' names are usually only transliterated into *kana* (Japanese characters) on name cards so local people can read them. Westerners' do not take a Japanese name. To do so makes the Japanese uneasy. Not so in Taiwan and China. Foreigners often choose Chinese names, but if you want one it must be chosen carefully: you will have it for a long time, it will leave an impression (good or bad), and may even say something rude about you if you are not careful.

There are two basic ways of taking a name, and help from a local is advised in either case. First you can transliterate the sound of your surname into close-sounding Chinese characters. For example, Smith is normally transliterated using the three characters, *Sz mi sz*. Many surnames already have equivalents and your teacher or friend can help you find yours.

If you want a new name in Chinese, then consider variations of the many names you will come across on a day-to-day basis. To spare confusion, the surname should perhaps approximate the sound of your original surname, while more whimsy can be used on your given name. Some examples are:

Western Name	Chinese	Meaning
Kirke Hart	*He Ke*	He overcomes
Mark Rabin	*Lei Peng*	Lightning *Peng* (mythical bird)
Chris Bates	*Bai Syau Ying*	*Bai* Dawn Eagle

We did have a friend, Mr. Gautier, whose name best transliterated into *Gwo Tieh*, meaning 'fried dumplings', so care must be exercised!

Red Ink

You have got your Chinese name and maybe even have a sample of your own calligraphy to seal. Now you need a 'chop'. The chop, or *jang*, is a personalized seal and is considered an indispensable accoutrement. Among the Taiwanese, Japanese, and Chinese it constitutes their signature. It is registered with the government and used on cheques, contracts, and other legal documents. Its historical importance is reflected in the massive size and ornateness of the emperors' seals on display in museums. It is guarded absolutely and much concern and dread is felt if it is lost. Advertisements must be run in the newspapers and one holds one's breath until it is properly de-registered or recovered.

As a foreigner, unless you manage a company or sit on a board of directors, you will probably not have a chop registered as your own. It does not stop you from owning one, though. They can be made in almost any neighborhood and common materials for a cheap one are wood or plastic. Larger, fancier ones are carved from stone and are frequently embellished with images of animals, perhaps your Chinese zodiac sign. Vermillion ink pads come with the chop, which has a notch or dot to indicate the proper orientation of the characters. Place the document or article to be chopped on a flat, preferably slightly cushioned surface (a desk mat is perfect), prime the chop in the red paste, then apply it to the document with even downward force. Rock it ever so slightly and remove it straight upwards. You have now made your mark as a Chinese scholar!

THE WEIGHT OF TRADITION

The long history of the Chinese people is a major source of cultural pride. It is the traditions that have sprung from this history that give the Chinese their identity. During the degradation of China, from the mid-19th to the mid-20th century, it was only China's traditions that sustained the self-respect of its people. Defeated both diplomatically and on the battlefield, robbed and torn asunder by corrupt and ruthless warlords, and exploited by empire-hungry nations from East and West, the Chinese people could only look to their past with satisfaction. By comparison, the present and future looked grim.

The same history, though, with its millennia of accumulated tradition, weighs heavily in the heart of all Chinese. It defines their social, familial, commercial, and political relations, as well as their relations with the spirit world and the physical universe. To deviate from expected behavior is to be labeled, stigmatized, harangued, and ridiculed. Taiwanese relate thoroughly and almost exclusively to their Chinese heritage, to the extent that when there is talk of *Tai Du* (Taiwan Independence), it is strictly political, not a break with cultural heritage.

American-born Chinese, for example, may either rebel against this tradition, or truly feel they carry it in their hearts. But, in any case, they will be seen as something less than full Chinese due to their upbringing—a source of frequent frustration for them when they wish to integrate into Chinese society. Taiwanese traditionally, and especially after the educational indoctrination of the Kuomintang, see themselves first and foremost as culturally Chinese (*Tai Du* sentiments notwithstanding).

One can become an enlightened barbarian by studying Chinese traditions, but never be accepted as a true equal. Some Chinese have asked foreigners, "Why do you want to be equal? Don't you feel superior anyway?" Because of inconsistencies in the Chinese heritage, a foreigner can always be told that he *bu ming bai*, in other words, he is not clear or does not understand the nuance of a cultural problem. This is a source of frustration that can be minimized if the foreigner studies with sufficient breadth and depth the Taiwanese cultural heritage. What is fascinating is that the three major traditions influencing the Taiwanese were all born concurrently, five centuries before Christ. One came from India and the other two from China.

CONFUCIANISM

Confucius was a scholar and philosopher born in the year 551 B.C. in Shandong, southeast of Beijing. In Mandarin his name is Kung Dz. He served kings and princes and is credited with the importance placed on education and bureaucracy by the Chinese. His school of thought was transmitted through several books known today as the *Analects*. They are very conservative. He taught the importance of relations and of the conscious effort required to maintain them. All people, all things, have a purpose and a station in life. If they all understand that purpose and station, and perform their duties well, there will be harmony. He softened this by stating that benevolence was the key to leadership, that in order to be treated well as a subordinate, one had to treat one's subordinates well. During the Song Dynasty (960–1279), a branch developed called Neo-Confucianism, which adopted the meditative and alchemic aspects of Taoism.

Confucian harmony, forced through the conscious exercise of 'proper behavior' (defined by someone else!), is the beneficial result sought by the philosopher and the king. If you do not understand your station and behave improperly, you have not been taught correctly. If

On Confucius's birthday, traditional rites include the waving of peacock feathers—symbols of respect and honor. The Chinese name for peacock (kungchywe) also includes the name of Confucius (Kung).

you willfully neglect your duties, you have been tainted by bad elements. For example, a wife who does not act 'wifely' or a prince who does not act 'princely' can severely disrupt harmony. The proper relation is one of subservient attention to the needs and edicts of one's superior (heaven, in the case of the emperor). This selfless devotion (*syau shwun*) can be compared to what the West calls 'filial piety', though, technically, this term is limited to familial relations.

Even today proper relations manifest themselves in the hierarchy of society and the respect that must be properly extended within the hierarchy: husband/wife, parent/child, teacher/student, boss/secretary, government/population, old/young, dead/living. Attached to these relations are expectations of behavior, rituals, gift-giving, and face-giving. There are young Chinese (perhaps in every generation since Confucius) who have chafed at the yoke of this tradition. They are labeled as 'unfilial' (*bu syau shwun*). Severe punishment has been used through the ages to bring children back in line so they will be 'educated' and not 'tainted'.

Another cultural result of Confucian tradition is the focus away from the self as the unit of society. In Western 'liberal' tradition, society is made up of individuals. Our solitary mythical heroes challenge nature and the gods (who themselves exhibit human foibles) and occasionally win. Not so in China. Sun Wu Kung, the Monkey King who accompanied Tripitaka on his trip to India to bring back the Buddhist scrolls, challenged the gods and as a result was punished by the Buddha, who put a gold band around his head. This band crippled him with pain if he became too cheeky. In Confucian society, you are a part of another unit, and don't you forget it!

The unit of focus adopted in Japan, Taiwan, and post-revolutionary China is different and the contrast is worth noting. In Japan, heavily influenced by Confucianism, the unit of focus has traditionally been one's superior and the group to which one belongs (shogunate, village lord, army, or–now–a company). In Taiwan, the unit of focus is the family. The family is self-regulating and controlled. Problems

97

are usually settled within the family, and the individual who has his or her own ideas should create consensus within the family before embarking on them. Consequently, the Taiwanese exhibit little civic-mindedness, the focus being on benefiting the family. To the saying, 'Charity begins at home' must be added '… and ends there'.

These units of social focus, group and family, are not all bad. Japanese corporations have a unity of purpose that is rare in the West, while Taiwan (as will be discussed in Chapter Nine) is a nation of family-owned enterprises. In contrast, the Communists in China, especially during the Cultural Revolution, tried to destroy the family as a unit of society to make society itself, under the cloak of the Communist Party (or, at the very least, the socialist work unit), the focus of society. Many are the perverse stories telling of children ratting on their parents during that era. Still today in China, when one calls for a person on the phone at his place of work, one will be asked "*Shenma danwei*?" (What unit?). It is possible that part of the disillusionment the young generation in Mainland China now feels is because their social unit is so ill-defined. Their tempestuous upbringing has neither prepared them to be individuals nor parts of clusters.

Confucianism is not a religion. There are, however, many Confucian temples in Taiwan and China, and there are various rituals and rites associated with Confucian obeisance. Many of these pay respect to him as the Master Teacher. Scholarship was as much the key to success in ancient China as it is in modern Taiwan, and the success of one's children is frequently prayed for. Think of Confucius as the patron saint of scholars, bureaucracy, and regimentation, and you will not be far wrong.

BUDDHISM

The Buddha, a contemporary of Conficius, was born a prince in northern India near the border with Nepal. In his youth he enjoyed princely activities such as archery, horsemanship, and statecraft. Still, he was not satisfied with life and sought a deeper understanding of the unhappiness he felt plagued mankind. This took him on a path that was to lead him through all manner of hardship, involving physical and spiritual testing. Eventually, having walked this bitter path, he achieved enlightenment. He told the world, through his disciples, that desire is the root of suffering and that man should compassionately tread an eightfold path in the pursuit of enlightenment. The path never ends until, after millions of years and rebirths, one finally gets it right and achieves enlightenment.

Buddhism spread from India to Sri Lanka and the Indonesian archipelago, north to Tibet, east to Burma and beyond. It grew into several schools, arriving in China in the first centuries A.D. Its popularity increased after the arrival of Da Mwo (Tamo or Bodhiharma in Japanese) who founded the Chan sect at the Shaolin

The seated Buddha and Chinese lions on Bagwa Mountain show how Chinese traditions have influenced Buddhism in Taiwan.

Temple around A.D. 500 His discipline included meditation, exercise and introspection. In Japan, and around the world, this school is more popularly known as Zen. The Shaolin Temple also was the source of one of China's most famous schools of martial art.

Buddhism is to China what Catholicism is to Europe, minus the Crusades and Inquisition. It fell in and out of favor with the emperors, controlled vast tracks of land and granaries of rice, and occasionally became a power unto itself, complete with intrigues and armies. It also made lots of money. In China, the Buddhist Pantheon expanded to include many helpers and hangers-on of the Buddha.

Whatever conception you have of Buddhism, you are almost certainly going to be surprised by what you will observe in Taiwan. Most Westerners' ideas about Buddhist discipline and serenity come from Zen austerity or Thai piousness. For the Taiwanese, Buddhism is a relief from misery and uncertainty. They will pray for mercy from Gwan Yin, the Goddess of Mercy, and then mercilessly pursue whatever end it was that created the conflict or unhappiness in their life. They will pray for a boy-child, for a rich husband, for a good entrance examination, for a gentler mother-in-law, not ever stopping to think that it is, according to the Buddha, their desire for these things that creates their uncertainty and unhappiness. The temples indulge this type of prayer, as will be covered in detail later in this chapter.

There are formal Buddhist monasteries and nunneries in Taiwan. Priests normally work out of formal temples which are supported by donations and benefactors.

Most hotels in Taiwan will have a copy of *The Meaning of Buddhism* in the bedside drawer, atop the Gideon's Bible. It is a good place to read about the general tenets of this popular religion.

TAOISM

Born several decades before Confucius, was a cantankerous ruminator named Lau Dz (Lao Tzu). A philosopher and librarian scholar at the imperial archives, his views were at odds with his king and he exiled himself. Legend has it that at the last mountain pass before leaving the realm, the border guard struck up a conversation with him and begged to be allowed to record his teachings. His words are passed down to us today in the *Dao De Jing* (also known as the *Tao Teh Ching*) and his philosophy is known as *Dao* (popularly spelled *Tao*), meaning 'the Way'.

The Western conception of Taoism is that it is based on quiet cultivation and respect for Nature. As with Buddhism, however, the casual observer will find that the reality of its practice in Taiwan greatly diverges from this conception. This is because, in Taiwan, there is both Taoism the religion (*Dao Jyau*) and Taoism the philosophy (*Dao Jya*). The distinction is important, though many Taoists in Taiwan might not admit it. The philosophers have traditionally shunned the priests who tried to create a religious expression of *Tao* to compete with Buddhism. Similarly, they shunned organized Confucian society. The philosophers, even today, spend their lives cultivating themselves privately and at higher levels in the seclusion of mountain hermitages.

On the other hand, the priests of the religion are itinerant and lead normal family lives, save when they have to don their red and gold robes, perform special rituals, exorcisms, séances, and the like. They do not lead celibate lives in monasteries. To the Taoist philosophical structure they have added numerous deities, spirits, and rituals which Lao Tzu had no time for. Though the religion has a cultural impact, its roots are in the philosophy.

Taoism the philosophy deals with change. It accepts that all things are in a state of flux and change is ceaseless. That is the 'Way of Nature'. The person who understands this, who can observe Nature without distraction, can thus move in harmony with Nature. To move in harmony with Nature is to tap its limitless resource. In their search to understand the Way of Nature, Taoists became perhaps the first empirical scientists. Through trial and error and recorded experimentation over hundreds of years and across various disciplines, they formulated basic scientific theories and practical applications.

Taoism is a practical philosophy developed by practical people who, in their search for health, longevity, and self-cultivation became many of China's most revered physicians, scientists, poets, artists, and inventors. It was only a Confucian geopolitical sense of superiority, coupled with the disdain for business and the self-seclusion of the Taoists, that prevented China from exploiting these inventions for greater global gain (the compass, gunpowder, crossbow, and porcelain, are just a few of their achievements). Taoist concepts permeate the everyday life of Taiwanese and it is worthwhile spending some time understanding them.

Taoist Physics

Though he is credited with the first succinct, if mysterious, statement of *Tao*, Lao Tzu was merely communicating principles that had been contemplated since the time of the legendary Yellow Emperor (c. 2700 B.C.) These were developed through an observation of Nature. From this Taoists surmised the beginnings of the universe in terms consonant with modern quantum physics. Three basic concepts to explain change relationships emerged.

In the beginning there was 'One'. One energy, one essence. This essence, the Prime Mover, is called *chi*. In humans, our breath is transformed into *chi* and we remain alive. A Taoist friend once described *chi* as the 'currency that maintains the economy of existence'.

This essence then divided into two, which became all things. The two are *yin* and *yang*. *Yin* represents yielding, declining, shadow, pulling, femaleness, emptiness, the hole rather than the donut. *Yang* represents aggression, expanding, light, pushing, maleness, fullness, the donut rather than the hole. Everything in the universe contains elements of both *yin* and *yang*. For example, a coin has two sides and if it is illuminated from one side, the other side will be in shadow. Water is yielding, yet over millennia even the face of the earth yields to it.

It was from the *yin-yang* theory that binary numbers were devised, thus setting the stage for all modern computer language. The interaction of *yin* and *yang* sets the stage for all the natural change we see around us: tides, wind and clouds, the rise and fall of empires, natural selection, $E = mc^2$.

The yin-yang symbol.

The Taoists further divided elements of change into five archetypes. These elements could be placed in a Cycle of Birth and a Cycle of Destruction, rather like a 'paper, scissors, rock' sort of sequence. Everything in the universe can be assigned an archetypal element to symbolize its change relation to other similar things. There are, for

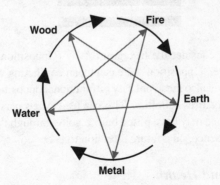

Generative (Circle) and Suppressive (Star) Cycles

instance, five types of seasons, emotions, flavors, colors, and senses. Even body organs are classified according to elements.

Finally, lost in the mists of pre-history, early Taoist sages, using the binary *yin-yang* theory, created a system of divination to try to explain and anticipate change. They devised a series of symbols to represent the system. Using one of several methods (such as drawing straws or flipping coins) to generate a random chance event, the diviners would classify the outcome as *yin* or *yang* and symbolize it with a solid or broken line. Three repetitions of the event created one of eight possible three-lined forms. These were called *gwa*. When repeated once again the combination of two three-lined *gwa* would produce one of 64 unique six-lined forms. Each six-lined form, known in English as a hexagram, corresponded to a phase of change and had an explanation attached to it. This system of divination was brought to the West in translations of the Taoist classic, *I Ching* (pronounced *Yi Jing*).

For example, consider the hexagram *Kwei* (Opposition) randomly selected above. 'Opposition' here can mean conflicting view points. However, it can also mean polarity or functional opposition, without which an entity loses definition. This can lead to new perspectives on the question one may have posed before going through the selection process and, hence, on a future direction to take.

Medicine and Health

Chinese medical theory, diagnosis, treatment, and prescription are based completely on the above ideas. In a healthy body, balance and harmony of the *yin-yang*, five elements, and the *chi* are maintained through proper nutrition (including nutritional breathing), activity, and quiescence.

- **Pulse diagnosis** classifies various pulses corresponding to several organs in a state of health, excitement, or decline. The Chinese physician will place three fingers on your wrist, feeling for three separate waves. He may look at your tongue, eyeballs, smell your breath, look at your fingernails. This, coupled with questions about your regular activities, will give him the basis for a diagnosis and prescription.
- **Acupuncture** (*jenjyou*) recognizes meridians throughout the body in which *chi* flows. In a completely healthy body, the *chi* flows smoothly to all areas. If, because of fatigue, stress, chill, or other pernicious influences, there is an interruption or diversion in the flow of *chi*, areas of the body may be affected. The acupuncturist, having made a diagnosis, will work to directly re-channel the flow of *chi* by inserting needles into the body. This will stimulate the affected point, or divert energy to the required area.
- *Twei na* (literally, 'push-pinch') is called acupressure in the West and works on the same theory as acupuncture, without intrusion into the body. It can nevertheless be mildly painful.
- **Cup therapy** (*bagwandz*) is interesting and rarely reported in the West. After an examination, the doctor will place glass cups with hoses and one-way valves on the patient's body. A vacuum will be drawn which sucks the skin in the chosen area and draws the blood to the surface. After perhaps five minutes, the cups will be cloudy with mist and drops of liquid will be forming on the surface. This is the negative *chi* being drawn out of the affected area. The cups are then rapidly removed (pop!), the skin is massaged, and liniment applied. Finally, the doctor might apply moxa (a bundle of burning herbs). These are gently stroked close to, but not touching, the skin. The patient will then be told to

quickly put his or her shirt back on.
- **Herbal medicines** are frequently prescribed. Each herb has its own properties, according to the table of the five elements. Different herbs will be prescribed, depending on whether you have, for example, a deficiency or excess of heat or wind. You might receive prepared powders to be taken with warm water, or you may be given raw herbs to be boiled down in a clay pot to form a strong-tasting decoction.

Traditional medical theory is understood on a folksy level by the average Taiwanese. You may be warned not to take cold drinks, to wear a T-shirt under your clothes, to get out of a draft, not to eat spicy things, to eat spicy things, etc. This advice will be proffered with the best intentions and is based on the common understanding of health promotion. It is best to thank the person for their advice, ask them for more information about the reasoning behind the thought, and reply that you will definitely take it into consideration. But note that, although thoroughly understood by physicians, not all people remember the reasoning behind their advice. It has become for them a kind of folklore of prevention and remedy.

Geomancy

As of late, Chinese geomancy has begun to get a lot of press in the West. In Mandarin the proper term is *feng shwei* (also spelled *feng shui*), which literally means 'wind and water'. It is the subtle art of crafting one's personal space to match one's mystic constitution. Properly choosing the direction one's bed faces, the elevation and position of one's house (relative to the natural surrounding elements), or adding the correct natural elements into an unnatural urban or office setting can motivate the flow of beneficial *chi* and discourage the entrance of pernicious influences. Health, wealth, and happiness may soon follow.

A Taoist geomancer can be employed (much as a diviner is in the West when searching for the location of a well) to help determine the best possible setting for your home or business, given the environment you have chosen. He will ask you some questions, walk the surroundings of your house or office, and frequently consult his *lwopan*. This is a round or octagonal wooden plate, with a compass embedded in the center. Radiating from the compass are lines (latitudes) intersected by circles (longitudes) which create boxes in which Chinese characters are written. At the periphery, there are 64 Chinese characters and hexagrams from the *I Ching*. By examining the direction of your setting, relative to surrounding elements and geography, he will determine whether good influences need to be brought in from one direction, or bad influences diverted from another. He may then prescribe modifications to the location of furniture (if you are lucky); the acquisition of some minor items, like a tree or aquarium (if things are not too bad); some structural modifications to the building, like changing the angle or hinge position of a door, putting a window where there is now a wall or vice versa (if the situation looks tough); or, at worst, recommend that you move or tear the whole building down (and it has happened!).

As a Westerner, your perceived lack of understanding of Taiwanese principles of life will be magnified. A Taiwanese boss who apparently lacks any knowledge of or belief in *feng shwei*, would be accepted by his employees, at least until some bad luck befell one of them or the company. But, behind your back or in front of your ears (in language you do not understand), your employees will be sizing you up for your sensitivity and knowledge of what might be important to Taiwanese. If you are looking for an office site with your assistants, ask about the *feng shwei* of the various options and seriously include it as a consideration in the final assessment.

Martial Art and Longevity Exercise

The popular martial arts of China have all been directly influenced by the traditional concepts described above and have, in turn, greatly influenced modern culture. You can observe Taiwanese, young and old, partake in these arts if you are willing to rise early and go to the public parks at about 6:00 a.m. Taoists believe that in the very early hours (4:00–5:00 a.m.) trees give off *ywan chi* or 'original energy'. This is the best time of day to do exercises and breathing that will absorb this energy. The bigger, healthier, taller, and older the tree, the better the breathing.

Tai chi for three!

Shaolin boxing came from the Buddhist Shaolin Temple. It is an energetic, comparatively acrobatic method, popular with the young. *Sying yi chywan* (*hsing i chuan*, or 'form and intent boxing') is based on the interaction of the five elements and is a focused, largely linear art. *Ba Gwa Jang* (*Pakua Chang*, or the 'Eight Trigram Palm') is based on changes exemplified in the eight trigrams and 64 hexagrams of the *I Ching*. The student of this art is trained to repulse an attack by using the power of circles and vortices. *Tai ji chywan* (*tai chi chuan*, or 'grand ultimate boxing') is based on the principle of perfectly matching one's motion to the opponent's *yin* and *yang* in motion. It is usually practiced very slowly and with deep concentration.

The above concepts imbue many aspects of life in Taiwan and China with a flavor the Westerner might find superstitious. They are best not treated as such. A modern, university-educated Taiwanese might nonetheless describe your post-teen acne problem as a manifestation of 'excess heat or fire'. Were you to go to a Chinese doctor and receive treatment, you might even be pleasantly surprised by the results.

All of the above traditions weigh on the Taiwanese in a *smörgåsbord* of spirituality. With some accuracy it can be observed that Confucianism dictates one's relationship with family (living and dead) and, to a lesser extent, with society; Buddhist beliefs dictate one's considerations of a personal afterlife and the need for compassion in this life; and Taoism indicates the path one follows in interacting with the world. There are other spiritual influences and manifestations and we will see that, in the temple, the *smörgåsbord* is replete.

The Lunar Calendar
Based on astronomical observations, the Chinese developed a lunar calendar of 12 moons. The Chinese word for month is *ywe* (moon). Because the traditional 'farmers' calendar' (*nungli*) is based on the lunar cycle, the dates of some holidays vary every year. The Lunar New Year is not on January 1, but falls somewhere between January

15 and March 15. Dates fixed by fortune-tellers as good or bad for certain activities are always expressed in *nungli* dates.

Chinese Zodiac

The Chinese zodiac is made up of 12 animals. Unlike the Western zodiac, which attributes one animal to one month, the Chinese zodiac attributes one animal to one year. The year begins and ends according to the *nungli*. The animals each have different strengths and weaknesses, different compatibilities with each other, and varying fortunes in each year. The dragon is the most auspicious sign. Read about the Chinese zodiac, understand your sign, and enquire as to the signs of others you meet.

Animism and other Spirits

Besides the well-known and formal religions and philosophies introduced above, there are countless other forms of spirit-worship, (some loosely connected to one or another school), which are said to influence the world of the living. Perhaps as an offshoot of Taoist religion, or because the Taiwanese were traditionally farmers and fisherman, spiritual powers are attributed to the earth in the person of Tu Di Gung, the Chinese god of the earth. By rice fields, tombs, and temples one will frequently see a small stone altar-chimney for use in burning spirit money in his honor.

Another important deity is Gwan Gung, the god of war. Befitting a world of military and industrial complexes, he is also the patron saint of businessmen. Beneath Buddha, Gwan Yin, Gwan Gung, and Ma Dzu (who is a protectress of fishermen and pregnant women) is a complete celestial bureaucracy. Every small town will have its own temple (or several), within which resides one of these 'divine ambassadors' who helps to communicate to the 'Big Boss' (usually one of the four mentioned above). This ambassador helps to keep tabs on the welfare of the pious.

Gwan Yin, the Goddess of Mercy, ranks high in the celestial hierarchy. Statues and images of her abound in Taiwan.

Another group of spirits said to have a direct influence over the fortune and health of the living are the disembodied spirits. Man is said to have two types of souls. *Pwo* is the *yin* component of your soul which resides in the earth (in the shadow) after burial. *Ling hwun* is the spirit which can go to Buddhist hell or be forced to walk the earth without a body after death. A neglected *ling hwun* can become a *gwei* (ghost or demon), or worse, an *e gwei* (hungry ghost).

Ghosts can wreak havoc on the well-being of the living. But what causes them to be neglected? In an application of Confucian thought to the afterlife, it is said to be a lack of attention to one's dead forebears, in the form of proper obeisance, feeding, clothing, and remuneration, that causes these astral beings to run amok. Family descendants are supposed to keep an ancestor tablet (with the deceased's name on it) and sometimes a photo of ancestors on the family

111

altar. As a minimum they should burn incense and make offerings. (For more about duty to dead ancestors, see information under *The Ghost Festival* in Chapter Eight and *Death* in Chapter Six.)

Trance Mediums

Taiwan has its own class of trance mediums, called *dangki* in the Taiwanese dialect. These men and women are usually chosen by the spirit of the locally-honored divine ambassador, mentioned above, to serve as a mouthpiece to the world of the living. They have no choice in the matter, sometimes trying to escape the responsibility by leaving town, but frequently surrendering to duty. Most small towns will not admit to having them, though they still exist.

When a person has a chronic and recurring problem and they have exhausted all other remedies, a *dangki* might be called in. Once in trance the problem is described and the spirit reveals the remedy. Perhaps a hungry ghost is settling into their lives until he or she is properly pampered. It might be the ghost of a girl who died in youth and never had a chance to get married who is causing trouble in her

A trance medium, or dangki, *performs Chinese martial art whilst in a trance during Matsu's birthday.*

spinsterly remorse. Though rare now, spirit marriages do take place in which 'forced' fate introduces a living suitor to the dead girl. Man and doll become wed in a formal ceremony. This has no legal effect, but the groom must now put the girl's ancestral tablet on his prayer table.

In the Temple

As you may have surmised by now, many temples do not serve only one deity or faith. There are dedicated temples to be sure, but it is also safe to say that most temples are heavily influenced by at least two of the schools introduced in the beginning of this chapter. So, what does a temple look like?

Unlike Western cathedrals, in which one can enter the great doors in the front and walk straight down the aisle to the altar, Taiwanese temples must be approached and entered through the side gates. This leads directly to a large open stone courtyard. From here you can clearly see the roof-line of the main wall and portals. The columns and roof-line will frequently have a dragon or dragons adorning it. Across the courtyard and up perhaps six steps, you will reach the threshold of the main portals, again not in the center facing the main altar further inside, but to the left and right. Painted on the massive doors will usually be fierce guardian spirits depicted in bright and realistic detail. You will have to step as much as one foot off the floor to cross over the threshold and enter the main temple courtyard area.

Think of all the architectural and ornamental detail you have seen so far as being 'security measures', just like a bank would install to prevent thieves from breaking in. Legend has it that ghosts cannot lift their feet over barriers, are not capable of making 90-degree turns, and must walk with both feet always touching the ground. Moreover, ghosts are afraid of fierce demons, or even seeing themselves in a mirror. No temple wants to be troubled by inauspicious spirits, hence the security measures.

Entering the main courtyard area from the right portal, you may see a window through which is sold incense, red candles, and spirit money. To your left is the main courtyard area. Taiwanese young and old (actually, mostly middle-aged or old women) are making obeisance and praying. It is a colorful, fragrant, and spiritually moving scene. Grandmothers are teaching children to pray and bow, one or two people might be crying, some are meditating. There is a solemnity not found in the street scene outside.

Dragons are auspicious symbols. This one helps protect the temple from evil spirits.

Prayer in the Temple

Depending on how serious the problem or how big the request, one might perform a simple or a complex obeisance. Let's walk through a full course. An old woman in front of you buys incense, a candle, and spirit money. She is carrying a metal plate with *lyan wu* (custard apples) on it, which she washed at a basin in the courtyard. She walks to a long table running parallel to the main portal wall. She puts the plate of food on the table as an offering. Other people have put down plates of various fruit, cooked chicken, and other food. She goes to the candle holders at each end of the table and lights one large fat red candle with gilt Chinese writing on its body, sticking the candle on an empty holder. She lights three sticks of incense in the flame of the candle and walks back to the center of the offering table, standing just behind a knee pad on the floor. She stands in prayer, with the three incense sticks held in two hands up at her forehead. She bows from the waist three times. She kneels, prays, and bows from the waist again three times. She rises and puts the incense in a brass censer about the size of a charcoal grill.

Walking to the side of the offering table again, she picks up two pieces of wood, the approximate size and shape of a wedge of apple. They are painted red; one side of each is flat and one side is rounded. (These are divining blocks. They are the primary method the Taiwanese use to communicate with the spirits and gods.) After silently asking the question on her mind, she drops the blocks. If they both land flat the answer is a 'no' (a 'flat refusal', if you like); if one is rolling around and one is down flat, the answer is 'yes'; and if both are on the rounded side, jiggling about, the spirit is laughing at the question—please rephrase it.

She walks down the steps to the center of the courtyard at the front of which is a huge brass tripod censer, well over a meter in circumference. Sweet plumes of smoke are drifting forth from its lid. Here she lights three more sticks of incense, prays, bows, and deposits the sticks into the censer. She goes up the steps into the main altar building which houses a gilt statue of the principal deity, bathed in red light with spiritual attendants to its left and right. She repeats the process with the incense.

She walks to a chimney to the far left of the main altar area outside the building. Inside it, a raging fire instantly consumes the stacks of spirit money she deposits into her spirit's 'cosmic savings account'.

Her prayers over, she goes to check her son whom she put in the study hall dedicated to Confucius in the row of rooms adjacent to the main altar area.

You notice several college-age girls enter the main courtyard area. They each burn three sticks of incense, pray, bow, and deposit the incense in the censer. Then they go to what looks like a large brass umbrella stand, filled with long thin sections of bamboo which are dark brown with constant handling. One by one, they gather the mass of sticks, lift, shake, and release them into the stand again until one stick stands out. This is removed from the bunch and the number on it remembered. When they have all had a turn they go to a wall of small wooden drawers which are numbered and contain colored slips of paper which have their fortunes written on them.

The temple is a community center facilitating communication with spirits. Communion is not normally sought, but rather help in solving some problem in the world of man. In this regard, people

The offering of fruit and the burning of incense are a typical part of prayer in the temple. You will also see such offerings on the street and in Taiwanese homes.

around the world are probably not so much different from the Taiwanese. We will explore in the next chapter how the weight of Chinese tradition affects the daily lives of your Taiwanese friends.

Chapter Six

RELATING TO YOUR TAIWANESE FRIENDS

"We had finished our warm-ups and basic drills when a little boy, about five years old, who had been looking at me, came over to stare at my arms. Without a word or a second thought, he pinched a mass of my arm hair and tore it out, then stared closely at the blond fuzz in his fingers. After completing his examination, he simply walked off."
—Chris's Diary, October 15, 1976, during a martial arts class in Taichung.

HOW DO TAIWANESE PERCEIVE FOREIGNERS?

Pride in their Middle Kingdom heritage directly influences how Taiwanese perceive foreigners. Ignore the fact that most Taiwanese are the descendants of farmers from Fujian during one of its poorest times; and ignore the fact that the major achievements associated with Chinese culture were not accomplished by the people of Fujian. It matters not. The emphasis on family ties, together with the indoctrination of the populace by an educational system based on their 'Chineseness' (serving to strengthening the ties to Mainland China for eventual reunification), inculcates them with a sense of cultural superiority. This colors how they perceive all others from outside the Middle Kingdom.

A tall, mustachioed American, conversant in Chinese language and mores, once attended a cocktail party. He entered into a conversation with the wife of a Taiwanese diplomat—a college educated, internationally traveled woman. She began to discuss how much further evolved the Chinese races are, as evidenced in their relative lack of body hair and smaller, delicate features. He proceeded to inform her of several ethnic, historic, and cultural facts in support of the premise that her view was utter garbage. Both people certainly left the encounter maintaining their original views.

Once your ear is trained and tuned to Mandarin, you may hear others call you various names. These epithets are used frequently and loosely. They do not denote bigotry in the sense of racial hatred, but they are used condescendingly, if unconsciously. All cultures create terms to demean or belittle that which they do not understand or are not comfortable with. The Chinese in Taiwan are no different.

Epithets—What They See Is What You Get!

Lau wai is the least offensive, perhaps most endearing, term. It merely means 'old foreigner'. Come to think of it, most Westerners do tend to comment that the Taiwanese look younger than their years, so

119

perhaps the inverse is true of Westerners. Another less benign term, which is frequently translated into English as 'foreign devil', is *yang gwei*. Westerners were very definitely a plague on the Qing emperor, during which time this appellation came into use.

Then there are also the physically descriptive terms. *Da bi dz* is common and means 'big nose'. This is given to Westerners who, by comparison with the Chinese, appear to have typically large proboscises. If you watch Mark Salzman's autobiographical movie, *Iron and Silk*, about his experience teaching English and training martial art in China, you will notice the large plaster cast nose he has attached to his dormitory room door. *Touché*! The final epithet is *ang mo*, as used in the Taiwanese dialect. It means 'red beards' and alludes to Westerners' relatively hirsute bodies.

These terms describe outward appearance. They tell us what Taiwanese find conspicuous about foreigners. "But I am blond/brown/black-haired, not redheaded!" you protest. It doesn't matter; you are still an *ang mo*. A foreigner's hairiness is a source of much condescension. They see it as being related to one's general level of evolution, body odor, neatness, and civility. Remaining clean-shaven and well-groomed will improve their impression of you. This also applies to women's leg and underarm hair.

Size

Though not singled out with its own epithet (that we are aware of), size is also a major concern of the Taiwanese when relating to foreigners. Their impression of Westerners is that they are BIG! Big noses, big beards, big torsos, big bellies (sometimes), otherwise big muscles, big bones, big limbs. In proper proportion, this might be attractive to the opposite sex (Taiwanese man to Western woman, or vice versa), but it is intimidating to members of the same sex. In the West, studies have shown that the majority of the top 1,000 company chief executive officers are over six feet tall. Size can be used at sales meetings, cocktail parties, or in the boardroom. And size and success usually have a correlation. Not so in Taiwan. The height of many chief executive officers falls around the five-foot six-inch mark. The foreigner who is bigger than the average Taiwanese should be aware that their size may be making those around them uncomfortable. In keeping with the local preference for humility in projecting oneself, this person should make an effort to physically bring him or herself down to the level of the people he or she is addressing. Sitting with the person, rather than standing, or standing one step lower on the stairs to talk are some techniques you might use.

Skin Color

Of course, the comments above relate mainly to Westerners, whose organizing capacity and modern technology the Chinese grudgingly accept were able to subjugate most of the world in the last century and bring the Middle Kingdom to its knees. But what about brothers and sisters from the African and Indian continents? It is sad to report that many Taiwanese view black or darker-skinned people even more condescendingly than they do the caucasian Westerner. It is generally felt that dark skin indicates a life of manual labor out in the sun. To avoid the stigma, Taiwanese farm women traditionally cover themselves from head to toe, leaving only the eyes exposed to the sunlight, even though the summer growing season in Taiwan is extremely hot and humid. They do not want to be tanned. Parasols are still popular.

Beyond this consideration, it is held that the African peoples have nothing to contribute to China, unlike the 'Western barbarians' who at least have technology, money, and markets. Until recently, one of the most popular brands of toothpaste in Taiwan was called 'Darkie' and its yellow tube had a black man wearing a top hat and beaming a bright white smile. Under pressure from race relations groups, the English name of the product was changed to 'Darlie' and graphic designers utilized more negative space in the drawing to obscure whether the person on the tube was black or white. But, tellingly, the

Mandarin name of the product remains *Hei Ren Ya Gau* (Black Man Toothpaste).

The Invisible Man

As obvious and extreme as Westerners' features seem to Chinese, they nevertheless are able to treat you as if you do not exist at times. This becomes even more apparent once you develop some fluency in the language. You might be sitting down at a table in a crowded fast-food restaurant and some local youths may sit down to join you. If they are especially polite they might have the gumption to ask you in English whether anyone else is sitting there. Otherwise, they may just sit down as if they haven't even seen you. But as they converse, the conversation will probably include some comments in Chinese about you: "Look at this guy. Do you think he can speak Chinese?" "Are you kidding! I have never met a foreigner who could speak Chinese." And so on and so on. Alternatively, you may be walking down the steps in an office building and pass two secretaries who comment on the *ang mo*.

In other circumstances, you might find attention being drawn to yourself, as Chris did when he spoke Chinese at a trade show exhibition stand. Although you are not invisible, it appears that the Taiwanese do not recognize you as a sentient being. They will poke their nose right into whatever you are doing or saying, crowd right up behind you, and maybe even proclaim loudly, "Hey, he speaks Chinese." Or, if you are unlucky enough to be involved in a road accident or other altercation, you may hear such unsettling comments as, "Hey, this guy's guilty/responsible/gonna get the electric chair!" Such statements are made as if you are not there to hear them.

We believe this behavior stems from several roots. Firstly, the Taiwanese truly do not expect you to be able to understand their language, even if they are commenting that you are speaking Chinese; and secondly, you are from outside their family, their neighborhood, their country, their culture, their lives. You are from a place which is of no consequence to them, but, at the time, present some momentary fancy, like an animal in a zoo.

Under such circumstances, it is best to keep your cool, remember the purpose at hand (selling, persuading, extracting oneself from a delicate situation, etc.), and ignore or try to befriend the 'peanut gallery'.

The flip side of this situation is when you walk into an empty shop and face the owner. As you enter, a look of mild panic drains their face. They are speechless. They do not want to lose face by not being able to speak English, but they believe it is futile to speak Chinese to you. They cannot ignore you, so what can they do? A few words in Chinese, no matter how badly spoken by you, will immediately return the blood to their faces, which will then sprout a smile. You have demonstrated an ability in their language, they know what they are dealing with, and can cope with it without losing face.

Relations with Ang Mos

Taiwanese preconceived ideas about dealing with foreigners should be noted. Because China has had an urban merchant class for several thousand years, they feel they are masters of the art of bargaining. The bargaining stance will constitute almost all relations that you have with Taiwanese, until you eventually become friends. Any informal relation has the capacity to include bargaining; with your workers, your landlord, anyone you buy products or service from. By comparison, Westerners are perceived as lacking. They are frequently taken to be overly honest, gullible, naive, and 'straight'.

'Gullible' and 'naive' translate into inflated prices being quoted at shops, which leads foreigners either to a lifetime of vigilance to prevent being 'ripped off', or the attitude that 'as long as the price is okay by my standards, I don't care if the shopkeeper made a healthy profit'. Regardless of the path you choose, congratulate the boss on his skill in defeating you after every transaction. She or he will respond by praising you.

'Overly honest' and 'open' means that foreigners express their true feelings too soon and too deeply. This sort of honesty will not be returned and can be embarrassing to the Taiwanese. It can lead to a loss of face (yours or theirs) and it can also be used against you by the gossipmonger. Reserve (but not cold stand-offishness) is seen as a virtue.

'Straightness' is another difficulty. This is related to the above. Making very direct comments, or even asking pointed questions and going right to the heart of the matter, implies impatience and a lack of civility. "Why didn't you finish the report yesterday?" might be better asked as, "Is there a problem getting the report finished?" If the answer is *"Meiyou wenti!"* (No problem!) then you can push for a commitment, "Good, I can have it within the hour, then." Now a problem may be revealed. Always probe deeper in a gentle manner, but don't take "yes" for an answer.

NOTE: If you show this book to a Taiwanese acquaintance and ask if the above perceptions of foreigners are accurate, they will consider the question too straight and will probably give you an emphatic "no" to avoid making you lose face unnecessarily.

LOW AND HIGH CONTEXT COMMUNICATION

Cultures tend to be divided into 'low context' and 'high context' varieties. This describes how people within the culture communicate. A low context culture means basically that people accept what is heard as what they will get. They do not seek secondary visual cues to support what is heard. America is described as a low context culture. When an American boss tells an American subordinate that his performance has improved and he is recommending him for a raise, the subordinate will accept the comment as a compliment and expect an increased paycheck in the near future.

In a high context culture, however, much is communicated beyond the words. Tone of voice, facial expression, physical proximity, body contact, hand action, eye action, and ritual all become part of the dialogue. If both parties are from that culture, both will understand that this unstated form of communication is taking place and they will end up with the same message. A fundamental stumbling block in cross-cultural communications occurs when people from a low context culture and those from a high context culture try to communicate, or when the meanings of visual cues and body language differ significantly between parties in the communication.

Taiwan is a high context culture. Much is communicated through body attitude, visual cues, symbols, and ritual (in the sense of prescribed action appropriate to the occasion).

FACE: GIVE AND YOU SHALL RECEIVE

Much has been written about face and the weight Chinese and Japanese put on it. The term comes from two Mandarin ways of referring to the physical face. A person can throw away or lose face (*dyou lyan*), or an action can be without face (*mei myan dz*). Curiously, one rarely refers to gaining face (especially for oneself). It is almost always referred to in terms of loss.

Face is the inexpressible pride one feels in oneself for one's station, education, employment, ancestry, family, and accomplishments; in short, pride in one's 'self-concept'. It is a subjective store

125

of value. Inexpressible because modesty forbids crowing about it; inexpressible because pride, conceit, and defeat are closely related to the Chinese. The Mandarin equivalent of 'pride before a fall' is *au je bi bai* (the proud one will be vanquished). One's face must be referred to indirectly and is best expressed in deeds, not words. A person who says he has great face is insecure and would be scorned by others. A person who, through actions, expresses greatness (at whatever is being done) has face.

Shame

Chinese culture is based on shame. This means that proper action is pursued lest it result in scorn being brought on oneself and one's family from others, who may be either family members or one's social group. This is inculcated from birth in the way the mother and father treat the child. It is the fear of losing face (feeling shame) that keeps people in line when they deal with others from their orbit. It also means that if they are around people from outside their orbit (i.e. foreigners and outsiders), they are relieved from caring about losing face. Hence, many actions that would be considered rude or low-class elsewhere (cutting in line, dumping garbage anywhere, etc.) are done with abandon when not near people known personally to the perpetrator.

The Hierarchy of Face

Another person's face can be referred to directly and generously eulogized. Take note, though; the Confucian hierarchies play an important role here. If you are in the superior role (boss, teacher, father, customer, etc.) it gives face for you to praise your subordinates. If you are in the inferior role (employee, student, salesman) your attempt to give face by praising your superior may label you a 'poseur' (not aware of your own level), or as someone currying favor. The Chinese have two colorful expressions describing this. A *gen pi chung* is a fart-following insect ('brown noser' in the West) who likes to *pai ma pi* or 'stroke the horse's ass'. Face can be given to superiors by letting them instruct you or give you face in front of others. They gain face by giving face, you gain face by retreating.

Confucian hierarchies of face are no more evident than in the definition of family structure through language. Every familial relationship extending out in several branches carries a distinct term. For example, older brother (*gege*) and younger brother (*didi*) are separate terms. Paternal grandmother (*dzumu*) and maternal grandmother (*wai dzumu*, literally 'outside grandmother') carry a distinct difference in tone and apparent class. The term for 'Mister' is most telling: *syansheng* means 'first born' (as in first-born male heir), a person with whom the hope and future of the family resides. In contrast, the term for 'Miss' is *syaujye*, which means 'little big sister'. If you are speaking English to your Taiwanese counterparts, you will not need to memorize all the different relations. However, you will need to remember how *you* fit into the hierarchy of face in each particular conversation.

One gains face by understanding the role one is in and what actions are appropriate to that role (in the Confucian sense) to maintain harmony (see Chapter Five). Much of the content of this chapter is devoted to giving you a feel for understanding in which role you might be perceived and what action would be appropriate.

Always Asking Questions

Taiwanese are very curious people and long to ask many questions of their acquaintances, friends, and guests. A short 'yes' or 'no' answer would be considered too perfunctory. If asked how your flight was, rather than just saying, "Fine, thank you" it is better to throw in some spicy details: "I think it was the best flight I have had. I was served some very good Sichuan-style shrimp. It was on time and the take-off and landing were as smooth as ice."

You may be asked some questions that you find intrusive: "How much did you pay for that?", "What is your salary?", "How old are you?" On the one hand, do not believe the questions are for the sake of just making conversation. They want to know as much about you as possible. It prepares them for the bargaining process. On the other hand, do not believe that a "None of your business!" type of answer will leave them satisfied or feeling good about you. It is best to say things like, "I got a very good price on it, but the merchant made me promise not to tell anyone", or "My salary is only adequate to begin to enjoy some of the wonders of Taiwan."

Equally important is how you ask your questions. Because of face, it is better to ask 'what', 'who', and 'how' questions rather than 'why' questions. For example, the question, "Can you tell me about the table in the parlor with the Buddhist statues on it?" allows them to explain their religious beliefs to you without bringing them into question. "How can I get a bus to Tienmu?" sounds better than "Why can't I get a bus to Tienmu?"

Almost Is Good Enough

Taiwanese will frequently settle for less than the ideal, perhaps because too much face would be lost if everyone went around asking to get exactly what they expected. This is best described as a Chinese boxing master told it to Chris.

Chris had learned a complex series of maneuvers from the old man which were supposed to begin and end standing in the same place. Somehow, after doing the moves, he always ended up one or two steps to the right. Chris asked the teacher to correct his moves so he could do it right. The teacher replied, "*Mei guan syi; Junggwo meiyou jywe dwei.*" (It doesn't matter; China has no absolutes). He went on to point out that before contact with the West, Chinese shoes had no left/right distinction; they could be worn on either foot. He cited another example of the emperor who, unlike in Japan, was not considered an absolute ruler. His power was based on the Mandate of Heaven and if he lost it (if the empire began to decay) he could be overthrown. Hence, from the emperor on down, nothing in China was absolute.

There are two other words used frequently to denote this easy-going attitude. *Swei byan* (at one's ease or convenience) is used as an answer to a question about structure or restriction, for example, "What do you want to eat?", "What should I wear to the afternoon tea?" However, do not take the answer *swei byan* at face value and expect only peanuts and beer, or cut-offs and slippers. It is a way the Taiwanese have of saying they are easy about something and have no expectations. Your host may still go to great lengths to make a delicious meal or dress up to the nines. If entertained by Taiwanese, especially in their homes, the host/hostess may frequently be heard to say *daiman* ((the food) was brought out too slowly) or *jeisye tsai chaode bu hao* (these dishes are not cooked well). As a guest, it is not your place to agree, but rather to exuberantly negate what she has said.

Secondly, *cha bu dwo* (not short by very much) means that the situation is *almost* what was expected. If a merchant or subordinate is saying this, he or she means 'it should be accepted as what was expected'. On the other hand, if you are asked if the item in question is what you want and you reply, "*Cha bu dwo*", it means 'no, it is not entirely what I wanted, so I expect room in the price'. Depending on the gravity of the task that was *almost* completed by a subordinate, together with your tone of voice to him and the words you surround it with, a *cha bu dwo* can give or take away face. It means either 'in the face of a very difficult task, you still managed to do it almost to absolute expectation', or 'the task was not difficult and you still managed to provide the work incomplete.'

As far as your own performance is concerned, 'almost is good enough' has its own manifestations. When Chris was studying intensive Mandarin in the United States 20 years ago, his Chinese professor told him, "No matter how long you study, no matter how good your Mandarin gets, when a Chinese says to you, 'My, you speak Chinese *so* well!', do *not* believe them." Indeed, even now, Chris might be conversing at a rapid clip with a group of Chinese strangers, when he senses that he has made a mistake. Invariably, they will choose that very moment to chime in Chinese or English, "My, you speak Chinese *so* well!"

This applies to all facets of Chinese culture which a foreigner is supposed to find difficult. When you drop your dumpling square in your lap, you will hear, "You really do know how to use chopsticks well!", sometimes followed by the telling, "Would you like a fork and spoon?" When you have ordered Sweet and Sour Chicken, Sweet and Sour Shrimp, and Sweet and Sour Meat Balls, no soup and no vegetables, you may hear, "You really do know how to order Chinese food!"

The point to this artifice is that they want to prevent you from feeling a loss of face. It is always inappropriate, however, to agree with their praise or make a statement to confirm it, such as, "Well, thank you. We use chopsticks all the time at home!" Conversely, if a Taiwanese host orders a meal for you which you find disagreeable, it is the height of ingratitude to say anything that implies he or she has not ordered well for you. Find something nice to say about the meal, even if it's only to comment that you have never sampled so many new and unusual dishes at one meal before in your life.

REN CHING WEI—THE KEY TO YOUR HAPPINESS

Ren ching wei is as important as face in getting along well within Taiwanese society, but little is written or said about it. That may be because it is not easy to pin down. It means 'the flavor of human emotions' and is best described as an attitude of sincerity appropriate to the role one plays, or else a charisma consistent with Confucian modesty. Those who have it are considered to be civilized and people are willing to do things for them. It is the positive feeling left with those you encounter because your message has been delivered effectively and in a 'high context' way.

A component of *ren ching wei* is clearly sincerity. When you had a visitor, did you offer them tea and pour them a cup anyway, even after they had said they did not want any? If you did not, your first invitation to drink tea was not really sincere. When you invite someone out, do you sound like you are really interested in going out with them and insist again that this is something they should do with you? If you don't, they may be left with the impression that you consider their company a necessary nuisance you would rather avoid.

A Chinese person will frequently turn down your first offer. It does not mean they do not want to participate. Confucian modesty dictates that they should not appear greedy or over eager. You must sincerely ask about three times to elicit the final response.

An example of this occurred when Chris, as a student, attended a dance party at a friend's house. He made two fatal errors in inviting the girls to dance, a task in which he did not ultimately succeed. Firstly, his question did not carry the proper role relationship, i.e. that of supplicant to the girl. He asked, "Do you want to dance with me?" "No," was the consistent reply. Better to have implored, "Please, dance with me." Secondly, he did not repeat the question, giving up after each refusal he received.

Of course, if after your third consecutive invitation, the person still says they have a reason not to participate, it is best to let off and insist they do this with you 'next time'.

Gift-Giving

The way of giving and receiving gifts is an important part of both face and *ren ching wei*, and it should be taken seriously. Different occasions call for different gifts to be given. However, the following should never be given:

- Knives or scissors. Sharp objects are not auspicious in Chinese culture. Giving any gift which is sharp or used for cutting suggests you want to cut off your relationship with the receiver.
- Clocks and watches. They are inauspicious; to 'send a clock' is synonymous with deliverance to one's final end. (However, one of Chris's business associates once gave him a beautiful cuckoo

clock, so this custom may be dying out. On the other hand, he could have received the clock from a foreign friend and wanted to be rid of it, hence returning it to another foreigner.)

- Handkerchiefs. These are associated with crying and funerals.
- Towels. These are a common gift to funeral attenders, so they have a bad association.

Gifts should be wrapped. The paper should be appropriate to the occasion. Red or gold are auspicious colors, but never just white, unless you are going to a funeral and giving towels away.

The ritual of presentation and receipt is important. The gift should be held in two hands, palms up if possible, and formally presented to the receiver. She or he should in turn use two hands to accept the gift, taking the time to look at and admire the beautiful wrapping, commenting on it all the time to the giver and the bystanders.

The person receiving the gift will usually not open it when it is presented. Urging them to do so will cause embarrassment. This is to preserve the face of all parties: if they are disappointed with the gift and it shows, you lose face; if the gift is better than those presented by other guests, the others lose face.

Though not opening the gift, they will chime with a chorus of 'you shouldn't haves'. This does not mean you shouldn't have. You should have! Giving a gift gives both of you face. The more generous the gift, the more face for you and the receiver. Do not skimp. An inappropriately cheap gift will label you as either a 'foreign devil' who does not know better, or even worse a 'niggardly devil' (*syau chi gwei*).

The Taiwanese are very practical people and gifts for rites of passage are frequently not purchased items, but cash. Except at funerals, money is always presented in even denominations in the ubiquitous *hung bau,* the auspicious red envelopes which often have gold characters on them. If a purchased gift is called for, then name brand or designer items are preferred because of the face they confer. Below we have listed some events that might call for gift-giving, along with the type and possible value of the gift to be presented. More information about ideal gifts can be found later in this chapter, under the individual sections on celebrations and rites of passage.

Occasion	*Gift*
House visit	Gift worth around NT$500–1,000
Graduation	*Hung bau* of NT$1,000, or engraved pen
Engagement	Cakes
Wedding	*Hung bau,* usually NT$1,000–2,000 from each person attending the banquet
New house/business	Paintings of propitious scenes (rice fields, fish, oranges, the god of wealth)
Man ywe (see below)	Gold
Man swei (see below)	Gold
Infirmity	Fresh fruits
Death	Wreath, canned goods display, or white envelope of at least NT$1,001

RITES OF PASSAGE

In the life of every Taiwanese are events which have profound significance and which call into play their most deep-seated feelings about their cultural traditions. They represent how your friends were raised and how they are raising their families. It is worth reviewing these one by one and understanding what they mean to your Taiwanese friends.

Childbirth

Pregnancy, childbirth, and motherhood are all very important to the Taiwanese. The extension of one's family is the only way to ensure that one will be taken care of in old age and in the afterlife. For a man, the birth of a son ensures the continuation of the family line and name, vital in Confucian thought. Family planning measures by the government have been successful in controlling population growth, except during particularly auspicious years, such as the Year of the Dragon, when they explode. (A Chinese friend once commented to Chris that he had hit the 'cosmic jackpot' by having twin sons born in the Year of the Dragon!) Because families are smaller than in decades past, even more attention is lavished on the mother and child than ever before.

The parents want to make sure the child gets off to the best start. This manifests itself in obvious and practical ways, such as eating nutritional supplements and highly nutritious foods during the pregnancy. However, other ways are more esoteric. A fortune-teller will be consulted to try to ascertain the most propitious date and time for the birth. Providing they are full-term, mothers might request to be induced or give birth by cesarian section at the appointed time. They will also consult the fortune-teller on the selection of a name. The fortune-teller does not select the characters, but rather tells the parents the propitious number of strokes the characters of the name should contain. Since the surname is never changed and the first character of the given name is usually the same for all the male or female children in that generation of the family, it means that the second character of the given name must be chosen carefully.

After being released from the hospital, the mother and baby will customarily go into one month of traditional confinement called *dzwo ywe dz* (literally, 'to sit for a month'). During this time, she will be physically inactive, except for feeding the baby. She is also not supposed to bathe or wash her hair (although now they surreptitiously do), and she will consume vast quantities of tonic foods prepared according to custom and Chinese medical theory. The most popular Taiwanese *postpartum* tonic is *ma you ji*, a whole free-range chicken cooked in a steamer in a combination of sesame oil and rice wine. All the cooking and tending were traditionally done by the baby's maternal grandmother, but *dzwo ywe dz* centers have now sprung up around the island to provide the service in a hospice environment.

Childhood: Man Ywe and Man Swei

Childhood begins when the mother and the baby come out of confinement at the end of the month. A banquet for family and close friends is held. The mother gets to dress up and go out for the first time in a month, perhaps display some jewelry she received from her husband for giving him a child, and the baby gets initiated in Chinese banqueting. Infant and mother mortality rates used to be quite high in China and this banquet celebrates that the mother and the child have survived the first crucial month. It is called *man ywe* (fulfilling a month).

If you are invited to a *man ywe* banquet, it is appropriate to give the baby a gift of 24 carat gold. There are many traditional medallions and wrist or ankle chains made just for this. Depending on gold price, they cost around NT$2,000–3,000. If you and your spouse are invited, only one gift is sufficient. It will come in a silken red and gold purse, so wrapping is unnecessary. If a friend has a baby but you are not invited to a *man ywe* banquet, do not feel put off. Buy a gift-set of baby clothes or accessories instead. To do so is very *ren ching wei*.

A similar banquet is held at the end of the first year on the date of birth according to the *nungli* farmers' calendar. This birthday is called *man swei* (fulfilling a year). By custom, a Chinese child is one year old at birth. At the beginning of the next Lunar New Year, the child is two. When you ask a parent their child's age, they may quote you the Chinese reckoning. If you ask an adult their own age, they will probably quote the Western reckoning.

When children are very young, they are almost commended for being naughty. It shows that they are lively and sharp (*jing*). They are doted upon, paraded around, dressed up, and played with by siblings and cousins. They are scolded now and then, but it is only to begin to imbue them with a sense of their own shame, their obligation to the family, and responsibility not to bring shame. As they near school age, however, there is an end to innocence. Life takes a sharp right-hand turn into conservative and regimented activity.

Schooling

The education of children is the very top priority for parents. After a brief working career prior to marriage, most women will settle down to either help in their husband's business and/or oversee the education of the children. Raising a family is practically synonymous with educating them. Such a high priority is placed on education because of the Confucian tradition. Under the system instituted in Confucian China, a government of career bureaucrats could all be tested within the system and achieve higher rank through further testing. Anyone, even a farmer's son, could hope to scale the ladder so long as an education could be provided. Education is seen as an investment in the future when the children will have to care for the parents in their old age. The medical professions or university level teaching careers are the preferred end-results, though high level business qualifications (overseas MBA) and technological science degrees (doctoral level) are increasingly popular. Couple this with an extremely competitive and exam-driven modern educational system, and you have a situation where children are pushed to study at all hours.

Schooling begins at the age of three when children enter pre-schools and special study groups for dance, music, gymnastics, and math. Parents will scheme to get their children admitted into elementary schools with better reputations. Most children enter first grade already able to add and subtract single digits in their heads, as well as write a handful of Chinese characters. Through *bu syi ban* (remedial study classes, or cram schools) parents may try to keep their children one year ahead of their actual study level. Nine years of free compulsory public education is provided. However, beginning with junior high school, the student must take a battery of tests to determine their aptitude and into which school they get placed. Competition is fierce for the best schools and students will cram all summer in preparation. Again, they will cram to get into a good high school and again for college. Those who do not get into university fall into other categories of schools, junior colleges and vocational-technical institutes.

A festival celebration provides a welcome respite for Taiwanese children who are very often pushed to study at all hours so they can achieve top scores.

137

Children are motivated to study hard through shame ("Aiya! Only 90 percent average on your test. Stupid!"), fear ("There is no way you can get into Tai Da University with these scores. How will you find a good husband?"), and physical punishment (Whap!). Teachers can strike students on the palms with rulers or make them *gwei swan pan*, literally 'kneel on an abacus'. Occasionally parents will use the carrot rather than the stick and promise a motorcycle or other inducement if the child tests into a certain level.

Schooling is based on rote memorization and is very strong in math, Chinese language and history, and the sciences. It is weak in creative thinking and problem solving.

Birthday parties for all but the first year of life are not customary, although with the advent of MacDonald's party rooms, the Western party is beginning to catch on. If you want to buy a gift for a friend's child, educational presents would be most appreciated. The parents' feelings about toys can be summed up: "They have no time to play!"

Bai Shr

During your time in Taiwan, you may wish to seek private tuition from an old master. This might be to learn any traditional art: calligraphy, painting, *feng shwei*, martial art, *chi gung*, medicine, opera, etc. Teaching was one of the most venerated professions in ancient China and to gain tuition from a traditional teacher requires one to approach him or her properly in a process known as *bai shr* (to make obeisance to the master).

It is best for the first meeting to be arranged by a Taiwanese friend, preferably one who knows the teacher. Take a gift for the teacher, but do not expect to see them at the first appointment. You may be made to wait or come back another day. If so, bring another gift for the second meeting. When you do meet the teacher, compliment him or her profusely and sincerely on the art you observe. The more favorably intelligent your comments, the better the impression left with the teacher. Do not expect to be accepted as a pupil at the first meeting.

You may be told that it is inconvenient, that the teacher does not have any pupils or no longer accepts them, or that the language barrier is too great. You are expected to persist to show your sincerity. You may be asked to train with a senior student instead. If you are already versed in the art and truly feel you can only benefit from the master's instruction, persist in your request. If not, ask the master to check on your work from time to time.

You may be told by other students about tuition fees. This is best given to the teacher in a red envelope. Eventually, if you are happy with your progress, if you like the teacher and she or he likes you, you may ask to formally *bai shr*. This means you are now a formal disciple of the master's lineage.

Courtship

The sexes are largely segregated throughout high school and mothers continue to preach the virtues of pre-marital chastity to their daughters. Pre-collegiate dating is more common than before, teen pregnancies do occur, and young men do rowdy things. But, in general, the problems that plague Western society, like promiscuity at a young age, drug abuse, teen gang violence, and graduates leaving school with no marketable skills, are not as extensive in Taiwan.

College is a time when those who have passed into the system relax. Once you get in, you can coast. The women remain more mature than the men at this point. Indeed, it seems that Taiwanese men mature only during and after the compulsory military service which takes place after tertiary education is completed.

Real dating and courtship begin after the priorities of education and career path are taken care of. Couples might have a first chance meeting at a social gathering, at a temple, during morning training in the park, or at the invitation of a friend. To be a matchmaker (*dzwo mei ren*) for a successfully wedded couple is considered very lucky. Taiwanese women plan for securing a suitable husband like a military campaign. They have a specific objective, specific tactics, and classically employ the least expenditure of their 'military resource' to gain the objective. There is tremendous face and security in bagging a good husband for oneself. Romance is a secondary consideration. Do not mistake this to mean, though, that shotgun weddings are common. In Mandarin these are described in the phrase *syan shang che hou bu pyau* (to get on the train first and then buy the ticket). To get one's husband in this way is a loss of face and shows no finesse.

A traditional concept, still much talked about (especially *after* one has met one's beau), is *yuan fen*, or 'predestined relationship'. This is the idea that certain people, young lovers in particular, are fated to meet and fall in love. Their paths are inextricably entwined. Mothers might look hopefully for some sign that this relationship was destined for their daughters. In our own case, the circumstance of our meeting in Taiwan leads us to conclude that *yuan fen* exists.

Like weddings, engagement ceremonies (here before the family's prayer altar) are increasingly elaborate affairs, involving great finery and expense.

Engagements

Engagements are increasingly elaborate affairs. Before they take place, the groom-to-be must approach the patriarch of the bride's family and seek her hand in marriage. Crossing this hurdle can be easy or hard, depending on how good a prospect the groom is. However, a token resistance will always be given to test his mettle and sincerity.

After this, an auspicious date is set, sometimes with the help of a fortune-teller, always according to the *nungli*. An engagement ring is normally given to the bride-to-be. Invitations to the wedding banquet, called *syi jyou* (joyful wine) are sent out, accompanied by a small gift, usually cakes.

Prior to the wedding day, the bride and groom will go to one of Taiwan's slick wedding centers. Taiwan is now a major exporter of fancy wedding gowns to the West and the local women take advantage of this. At a wedding center they will be shampooed, trussed, made-up, filled out, dressed in many varieties of high fashion outfits, and photographed at each stage of the magic to preserve their beauty at that moment for posterity. It is truly amazing what these artists can do with the raw material that comes through their doors. Location photography is also part of the package. As much as U.S.$2,000–3,000 might be invested in this extensive collection of portraits and framed poster-sized pictures.

Weddings

The big day arrives. The wedding might be held in a church, at home, or at Taipei's City Hall. Less time is spent in planning the exchange of vows than the banquet. The banquet is a very big event, very important, and much face is attached to it. It is paid for by the groom's family. The size of the banquet is measured by the number of tables required, each seating 12 guests at a cost of between NT$12,000 and the sky's the limit! This price is per table for a set banquet menu not including drinks. An average-size banquet might require 30 tables. Bookings for the best menu at the best restaurant that can be afforded must be made well in advance for auspicious days.

The *Hai Ba Wang* (Ocean Emperor), prominently located at the corner of Chungshan North Road and Mintsu East Road, is an example of a banquet hall that caters to weddings. Formerly the Roma Hotel, all 12 stories were converted into a restaurant with private function rooms. Business is booming and they have set up branches in many locations.

The grandparents and parents of the groom and the guest of honor normally sit with the bride and groom at the head table, always located furthest from the entrance, next to a wall. Behind the table on the wall is a red neon light or silk banner with the 'Double Happiness' character (*Shwang Syi*) on it. At other tables will be seated friends and business associates of the groom's parents, relatives from both sides, and you perhaps. For a description of proper dining and banquet etiquette, see Chapter Seven which deals both with casual and banquet dining and drinking.

You will need to bring a cash gift in a *hung bau* for the newlyweds. The amount will vary depending on their relation to you. You should give more if one of them is a subordinate, a very special friend, or the child of an important business contact; less if they are just a friend. The *hung bau* should contain at least NT$1,000 for each person you bring with you. If you and your spouse attend, that means NT$2,000. At the entrance to the *syi jyou* will be a table, perhaps covered in a bright satin cloth, on which people are writing names. The people at this table are accepting, counting, and recording the *hung bau* given by guests. A *hung bau* is expected even if you are the guest of honor— an even larger amount perhaps.

During the dinner, the newlyweds will go from table to table and toast each group of guests. Otherwise, the toasting at each table will be according to the description in Chapter Seven.

New Houses

Taiwanese friends of your acquaintance may at some stage buy a new house. As with people the world over, this is a big event for the Taiwanese. They may have a housewarming party or a banquet. If they have a party, or you are invited over to see them soon after they have moved in, it is appropriate to bring a gift. Mirrors, pictures, paintings, and so forth are acceptable. Never send a clock (see the section in this chapter on gift-giving). If you know which household appliances they are lacking, you might send one of them.

New Businesses

Many Taiwanese prefer to be masters of their own fate and often leave employment with others to start their own company. If your friend and business associate starts a new business, branch, or factory, it would be appropriate to send a gift. Again, mirrors, pictures, and paintings are appropriate, but this time the gift may be ascribed to you or your business. This is often painted on the mirror or picture. If a sample of calligraphy is commissioned by you for the occasion, it may be attributed to you.

The Taiwanese most frequently pray for success in their undertakings. When moving house or opening a new business, suitable prayers to the gods for prosperity will be made in the temple.

143

Infirmity

Illness is a touchy subject. It is not considered good manners to say to a friend who has otherwise proclaimed to you that he is in good health, "Really, I don't know, you look a little pale to me" or, "You really should have that mole with the hair growing out of it looked at." To make such statements is to wish the ill that you are implying on the person. Discussion of preventative maintenance is similarly frowned upon, so, however good your intentions, don't say things like, "If you don't cut down on the cholesterol you're going to wind up with a heart attack."

Discussions of wills are also sensitive, but the custom is that all undesignated property goes to the oldest surviving male in the family.

Some people might even find a discussion about the purchase of life insurance rather touchy. Such insurance is a growth business in Taiwan, but it seems that the selling strategy used by the insurance companies is to turn the policy into a bet of sorts, and Taiwanese love to gamble: "We bet you won't live X years. If you do, we pay $Y. If you don't, well we pay $Z".

When a person does take ill with a serious affliction, it is not uncommon for the family to approach the best specialist in the field and beg them to treat their relative. Gifts and red envelopes have been known to trade hands to get the needed appointment for surgery. If the doctor were to decline to take the gift on moral grounds (Hippocratic or Hypocritic Oath?!) they would lose stature and face. They might be magnanimous and say they will do it cheaply or without being paid because they are a nice person, but, should the relative survive, the family will still try to bestow the gift on them.

If you are made aware that a person has taken seriously ill and would like to see you, then by all means make the effort to do so. Talk about pleasant things: hope, recovery, your last golf game. Nice books or magazines, cassette tapes, or special foods and fresh fruit are appropriate. Another alternative is a living plant for long-term illness, but do not give cut flowers as they are used at funerals.

Funerals

Sadly you might be called upon to attend the funeral of a friend during your stay in Taiwan. Funerals are a time when everything you have so far read about Taiwan comes into play: Confucian ethics and filial piety, face, traffic, the high price of land, *feng shwei*, money in envelopes, communication with the spirits, *ren ching wei*, everything. You will certainly observe funeral processions during your stay in Taiwan. You may even be invited to participate in one. Even if you are not, it is important to spend some time understanding the beliefs behind funerals because, in Taiwan, how people die is a key to how they have lived.

Funeral customs vary between the Taiwanese and the *Wai Sheng* peoples. They are somewhat subjective and very extensive. Let's walk through a typical upper-middle-class death of a patriarch, realizing that variations on a theme do occur.

Mr. Su dies at the age of 54 from a massive heart attack brought on by years of eating a lunch of stewed fatty pork on rice with a hard-boiled egg. He never even makes it to the hospital because the ambulance is delayed by afternoon traffic. He did not think himself ill, has no insurance and no will.

His wife is bewildered and not sure what to do, but well-intentioned relatives begin to tell her. Unfortunately, they do not agree on what would be the appropriate face to give her husband and she is soon made more upset and confused. Her son, 20 years old, gets leave from the army to help prepare the arrangements with her. In their mind, there is no question that Dad must be buried rather than cremated— no face in that. So they request the body to be transferred to a funeral parlor on Minchuan East Road. They pick out a casket—a fine hardwood model hewn from one log and with the traditional rounded sides and lid.

The body is dressed in many layers of clothing, six in his case. Clothes of natural fibres are preferred because they decay at the same speed as the body. The casket is brought to the Sus' home and a final

145

viewing of the body is held. Then the casket is closed and painted. The paint acts as a seal to keep the stench of decay confined.

Tradition requires that mourning take place for 49 days (seven days a week, for seven weeks). Because they have a ground floor unit and can afford to do so, Mrs. Su opts to keep the casket in their parlor, which is converted into a place of mourning. A white sheet is suspended around the casket area and a prayer table with a brass censor and candlesticks is placed in front of it. Condolence gifts begin to arrive from friends, relatives, and business associates. These are either wreaths of artificial flowers with a message penned on a center circle of paper, or pyramids of canned foods, beer, boxes of monosodium glutamate, and rice wine. These also have messages attached.

Through the weeks, people visit to chat with the family, burn incense, ask about how the funeral plans are going, and throw in their unsought opinion about how the funeral should be handled.

Mrs. Su has asked her son and her husband's younger brother to pick out a burial plot. This is no mean feat. They must find a plot that has acceptable *feng shwei*, is reasonably accessible for the yearly tomb sweeping, is allowed to be used for burial, and is affordable. For two days they search through the hills and valleys around Gwan Yin Mountain (just across the flood plain southwest of Taipei), talking to farmers, mountain men, tombstone carvers, and funeral directors. They finally find a suitable location, but the asking price is NT$1,125,000 for an elevated piece of earth 36 feet wide and 36 feet across, with a view of a valley. Fierce negotiation takes place and they finally wrest the plot for NT$1,100,000. Quotes are obtained from stonemasons and landscapists. Designs are weighed and selected.

Burial in an expensive plot is not the only alternative. Cremation is also fairly common. For a fee, the ashes might be kept in an urn in a labeled wooden locker at a temple. Monks will occasionally burn incense and perform rites. However, this final resting place is normally reserved for those who died young or ignominiously, or where the family truly cannot afford the expense. In Mr. Su's case, neither applies.

The son and brother are expected not to shave during the mourning period. It reflects their sacrifice of personal material comfort, although, in modern Taiwan, some men opt for just growing a moustache during this period or even continue to shave. The men and women have all used a safety pin to attach a small piece of black cloth to their shirts and blouse sleeves. They also eschew brightly-colored clothes during this time, especially lucky colors like red. To wear them would be symbolic of celebration over the loss of the family member.

Meanwhile, plans for the funeral are under way. The guestlist is drawn up and announcements printed on white cards are distributed. Mr. and Mrs. Su are nominally Buddhist, so some monks specializing in funeral chants must be hired. The funeral reception area has been extended out the front door and into a tarpaulin-covered area in the street. They have talked nicely to the local police constable to beg his forbearance and have sent a little card of apology to the neighbors for any inconvenience.

On a chosen day, several weeks before the funeral, the immediate family gathers to perform a *bai bai* (a ritual obeisance). Mr. Su's youngest sister, 30 years his junior, has just got married within the month and she is excused from all the ceremonies. During these grim affairs, relatives judge one's grief by how loud one sobs and how drained of tears one becomes. Traditional Chinese oboe and cymbal music, together with chanting, can be heard. At specific times, certain members of the deceased's family are expected to come forward, bow, kneel, prostrate themselves, kneel, stand, bow, and repeat the process three times. This is known in the West as 'kowtowing', but it is is actually pronounced *koutou*, meaning 'to knock the head'.

Seven weeks after the death, the family has another *bai bai*. This time the accoutrements necessary in the afterlife are made in paper miniature and burned after making an offering. Bales of spirit money, metallic paper Mercedes Benz cars, paper clothes, houses, *mahjong* sets, everything the well-heeled man with lots of time on his hands (an eternity to be exact!) would ever need. The spirit money is for those sundry expenses he is expected to run into. The fires of hell burn cooler and the doors to heaven open easier with a little grease.

On a different day, a *bai bai* is held for more distant relatives, friends, and associates to participate in. This may also take place on the day of the funeral. On this day, the family performs an obeisance again. Traditionally, Taiwanese would dress from top to toe in coarse white fabric and burlap, and wear rough woven rope sandals on their feet. This, again, is a symbol of grief and the sacrifice of personal material comfort. The Su family have opted for just a hood and cape of burlap worn over street clothes during the prayer and final tears over the coffin. One, two, sometimes three musical troupes will be playing during the funeral. They have employed just one.

You were a friend of Mr. Su's and have been invited to attend. At the funeral, similar to a wedding banquet, will be a table to leave money. This should be in a white envelope, not a red one. An odd amount, in excess of NT$1,000 is recommended. Follow the lead of those near the casket. Approach the person handing out incense and pay your respects. Feel free to ask questions. You may take photos, but ask first. You will be welcome to go all the way to the burial site, but it is not expected.

The family and friends accompany the bier from the residence to the funeral wagon. This brightly decorated truck has row on row of orange, yellow, and green plastic flowers. Above the cab is a photograph of Mr. Su and his name. The family accompany the casket on this truck, followed by a procession of trucks with bands, participants, and scores of plastic flowers. The procession goes around the deceased's neighborhood, his old haunts, and then heads out to the burial ground. If the procession gets stuck in traffic, there is some concern because the coffin must go into the ground at the specific time chosen by the fortune-teller.

The relatives and friends will help to carry the coffin to the burial place. A fortune-teller has provided a list of which zodiac animals

Hundreds of former students pay their respects by escorting the coffin to the bier at the funeral of Hung Yi-hsiang, Chris's renowned martial arts master.

should not actively participate in the ceremony, so people born in those years must just observe the proceedings.

One cousin of Mr. Su's, who pretends to be an expert on *feng shwei*, saw the burial ground after it was bought and declared that the *feng shwei* was bad. His implication was that the family were being unfilial. To counter this, Mr. Su's son and brother have hired their own *feng shwei* expert. He declares the site sound as they put the casket in the ground and he instructs them on how to precisely align the box according to geomantic forces.

Before covering the casket with earth, it must be cracked open to release the spirit within and to admit a fresh supply of oxygen to help the corpse decay. All participants are asked to turn away from the coffin when this is performed. It is considered bad luck to look.

There is a tradition in China that, after eight to 12 years, the remains are exhumed. The bones are scraped clean, dried, and arranged in a special way in an earthen pot. They can then be stored at the burial site in a small mausoleum. We have also heard this is a *Wai Sheng* custom, adopted by those who hoped to return to Mainland China after their deaths.

After the casket is buried, spirit money is distributed and burned, and hard-boiled duck eggs are given out. One traditional custom was for a hard-boiled duck egg to be placed in the casket with the dead. The implication was that only when the egg hatched (i.e. never) could the deceased come back to haunt the living. This custom is modernized at Mr. Su's funeral, where the eggs are consumed at the site and the broken shells scattered over the grave.

RELATIONSHIPS

It should be clear by now that tradition, based on the guidelines laid down by Confucius and his followers thousands of years ago, is still influencing how the Taiwanese live their lives. This also applies to all kinds of relationships that exist amongst the Taiwanese. However, the fly in the ointment here is modernization. Whether the Western liberal tradition is to blame, as many social critics trumpet, or whether this is the inevitable direction that a people take when faced with industrialization and departure from the farm, is a debate sociologists can take up. But change is taking place and where old and new continue to chafe, sparks will inevitably fly.

Familial

In the family, this change frequently manifests itself as children who do not *ting hwa*, or 'listen' to their elders the way they are supposed to. The old complain that the young grow up, leave home, and do not care about them or for them. Continuing the shame-based culture, they lay a 'guilt trip' on their children. In one respect, it is fortunate that the remnants of the extended family still prevail; it means the elderly are cared for by their children. There is no mandatory social insurance in Taiwan, so children must hope their parents have savings, or be prepared to take them in. On the other hand, parents frequently invest their savings in their children's education, with the explicit expectation that they are making an investment which will provide a return to them in their old age.

Gender roles are also affected by modernization. Women work more and for longer hours, and they have greater expectations of freedom and voice in marriage nowadays. Women's rights have been protected by law since the 1940s, but it is very difficult to legislate equality when half the population does not agree with it and the other half is not in political control to enforce it. For sure, the situation for women in Taiwan is better than it ever has been and most women are content with the pace of change. Men trying to cope with the change find that old role models do not work anymore. Some are left confused and frustrated. Divorce, considered to be evidence of the weakness of Western values, is consequently on the rise.

Sexual

Sexuality is also changing. While rather reticent when it comes to discussing sex, the Chinese are not prudes and have a long and colorful history of sexual techniques, experimentation, and enjoyment. Sex is neither something to be displayed, nor is it something to be ashamed of. It is natural, it is enjoyable, it is not sinful, and it is the act that brings family and future to the world.

Traditionally, premarital sex was not unusual, if you include concubinage (which is now outlawed but still practiced informally). But the concubine could never compare herself to a 'number one' wife: she had no rights, her children were not the heirs of their father, except through special circumstances, and if her 'master' died, then she was chattel to be exhausted or disposed of. Not all concubines ended up this way. Empress Wu Hou started at the bottom rung of the ladder in the imperial household in the 7th century A.D. She was so beautiful and skilled in bedroom arts (as well as scheming!) that she became the emperor's concubine. When he died, she became his son's concubine, eliminated his first two wives, ascended the throne by his side, saw his death, and then became the first empress of China! She was, by historical accounts, an able ruler but she had such a voracious sexual appetite that she apparently exhausted to

151

death many of the men sent to please her.

In normal life today, mothers hope that their daughters might marry a kind, well-to-do man and become his 'number one'. That means saving herself for him on their wedding night. Chinese mothers even today perhaps equate premarital sex with concubinage, or letting the man sample the goods before he has made a commitment, thus spoiling the girl's chance of finding a 'good' husband. They consider easy virtue to be a poor bargain—stupid but not sinful.

Young couples in Taiwan do engage in premarital sex and occasionally move in with each other. Among more traditional or rural families, if this is discovered, the young couple may be forced to marry, even though the girl is not pregnant. More frequently, in modern city families, it is tolerated, but with a chorus of laments from mama.

Inter-racial couples certainly exist, both Western men with Chinese women and vice versa. Such couples must overcome the regrettable stigma attached to Westerners—the legacy left by the United States military after their use of Taiwan as an R & R outpost during the Vietnam War. Chinese women seen casually with Westerners at that time were irredeemably equated with whores, whether they were or not. Even recently, this meant that women who married Westerners had to maintain a very proper bearing in public, or be frowned upon by society. It was not until the 1980s that young women seemed to partially liberate themselves and could be seen relaxing with foreigners and having relationships with them. One would doubt, though, that they would ever admit such a past to a future Chinese husband.

What about homosexuality? It is illegal in Taiwan. It is also proscribed by Confucian ethic. It is considered to be against the 'Laws of Heaven' since no progeny can result from such a relationship. No progeny means no one to worship one's ancestors or oneself when one dies, which means an eternity as a hungry ghost. Taoists are more practical about it. The sexual union of man and woman is a mystical, energetic bonding of *yin* and *yang* elements. It is healthy and restorative when properly consummated. They believe it is difficult for the homosexual union to approximate that transfer of energy. Nevertheless, homosexuality and lesbianism are slowly emerging from the closet in Taiwan.

Friendship

Lifelong friendships among the Taiwanese seem to evolve between 17 and 24 years of age. During this time, young people are entering college or vocational training, going through military service, and establishing a career. The friendships Taiwanese establish at this time, when they are first breaking away from the confines of the family, seem to be the ones that last into adulthood.

As for making friends with Taiwanese yourself, the best advice is to be sincere and aware. Try to understand what your social relationship is with the other person, act within the observed bounds of that relationship, but continue to strive for an increasingly sincere and communicative friendship.

THE HOUSE VISIT

Unlike in Japan, it is very possible that you might be invited to visit the home of a Taiwanese friend. This will be a nice opportunity to get to know this person's family better and learn more about the daily life of Taiwanese. They will certainly be lowering the curtain for you, revealing more of their inner lives to a foreigner, so it is important that you make them feel comfortable about what has been revealed.

If you are invited over for a dinner, it would be appropriate to bring a flower arrangement, or a bottle of whiskey or wine. Present this to the person who invited you.

Remember that in most Taiwanese homes, the wearing of street shoes is not permitted. Always make the motion to take your shoes off. Only if the host insists that you can wear them inside should you do so. If asked to remove your shoes, you may be given slippers to wear.

You will probably be led into the living room (*keting*) to meet everyone. Acknowledge the oldest person first. Greet them and get introduced, then do the same to the other people present. Expect a fuss to be made over you. Do you want a drink? Do you want a snack? Was it hard to find this place? Are you hungry? Are you thirsty? Do you want a cigarette? Here's some tea for you. Here are some snacks for you. Please sit. Don't stand up on my account.

You will hear the phrase *bye ke chi* (don't assume a guest's airs) repeated again and again. In other words, make yourself at home. Relax, but remain courteous. Accept this attention with good-natured gratitude, as if you are unworthy.

If there are children, they may come over to have a closer look at you. Talk to them in Mandarin or English. It is bound to provoke a reaction that will lead to some laughter. Taiwanese love children and if they see you relaxing with them, it breaks the ice. Unless you are very close to this family, though, it is better not to hug or have the children sit on your lap. Anyone whom you have not met before is bound to ask a lot of questions (as discussed earlier in this chapter), so be prepared.

A Note on Bathrooms

During your visit you may need to use the toilet. There are several things to note. Many apartments in Taiwan have only one full bath. If that is the case, you may find a whole family's toiletries in there. Because of the location of drains and hot water, you might also find the washing machine. The floor will frequently be wet. Take all this in your stride. Before you enter the bathroom, you may be asked to put on a different set of slippers. These are plastic bathroom slippers. They keep your feet dry and prevent you from slipping on the wet floor or getting your other slippers wet. Do not wear your house slippers in the bathroom or vice versa.

There are two varieties of toilet in Taiwan. Most apartments are now equipped with the Western-style 'sit down' toilet. Especially when outside the home, though, you may find a Japanese-style 'squat' toilet instead. These take some getting used to. Squatting is, however, the most natural and 'ergonomic' position for bowel movement. Without going into indelicate detail, suffice to say that you face the drain-cowling of the toilet, place your feet on either side of the chasm, and squat. Make sure your cuffs are not in the way and have your toilet paper ready.

Most toilet paper for home use in Taiwan is not on rolls. It comes in plastic bales pre-cut into approximately 10 by 10-inch single-ply sheets. These are normally kept in a vinyl box on the cistern lid. Return unused paper to the box.

If you are staying for an overnight visit, you may want to take a bath. Taiwanese homes do not have central water heaters. They utilize wall mounted gas or electric spot heaters that heat water only when turned on and activated by water flow. If you have any questions, ask your host.

Also note that many Taiwanese homes do not have a bathtub. They have showers with no specific cubicle, the water going down a drain in the floor. They do not usually take long steamy showers. Traditionally, the Taiwanese would fill a large plastic pan with water and use a dipper to ladle water onto themselves, soap up, then rinse off with the remaining water. In today's world of decreasing resources, this is probably the most environment-friendly way to bathe. By looking at the facilities available, you will be able to figure out what the appropriate bathroom etiquette is. For instance, if you have left soap suds or hair on the floor, rinse it to drain them away. Do not worry about getting the floor wet!

We advise you to bring your own towel if you go to a Taiwanese house for the night. Taiwanese will normally only keep one small towel per family member and this is usually the size of a kitchen towel. It is quite thin and is used for both washing and drying, being wrung out in between. You will not find a closet full of thick fluffy white cotton towels here.

Coming and Going

Lastly, if you are staying as a long-term visitor with a Taiwanese family, keep the following in mind. They know you are a stranger in a strange land. Hope for your own sake that they feel some responsibility for you. Normally they will, so you should not unduly worry them by disappearing for a night, or leaving for the afternoon without letting them know where you are going and when to expect you back.

–Chapter Seven–

CUISINE OF THE ILHA FORMOSA

Eating constitutes a major preoccupation, concern, and form of enjoyment in Taiwan. You would expect this coming from a nation that has had its share of famines, hard times, and over-population. In Mandarin and Taiwanese a way of asking, "How are you?" is to enquire, *"Ni chr bau le ma?"*, meaning literally, "Have you eaten your fill (yet)?" Happily, food is now plentiful in Taiwan and both Taiwanese and *Wai Sheng* chefs are masters at its preparation.

Once you are settled, you will definitely want to get out and about

157

and enjoy at least some of the vast variety of food available. But, before you venture into Taiwanese restaurants and hawker centers, you should be prepared for what to expect. There is one word that describes what Taiwanese seek in dining and entertainment. That word is *re nau*, which translates directly as 'hot and raucous'. This means that, while Westerners going to a French restaurant will seek a quiet repose, Chinese going to a restaurant are looking for noisy, happy diners enjoying their repast and the company of friends. Loud and sometimes aggressive toasting takes place. The noise of the food being prepared in the kitchen is heard clearly in the dining room. The plates and bowls being removed from a neighboring table clang and bang. All of this is part of the enjoyment.

Some foreigners take umbrage: "Why can't I just enjoy a quiet meal out?" Go to an expensive Western restaurant, then! For the Taiwanese, *re nau* is part of the enjoyment of eating and being alive. If they had to eat a Chinese dinner in regimented silence, they would not be happy. We had some Canadian friends who had lived in Japan for 10 years and had become immersed in the formality of the culture. We went with them to a Japanese eatery in Taipei. The *lao ban niang* (manageress) came over and served our tea and appetizers, banging the cups and saucers on the table in a happy rush. My friend, who was used to the formal, non-obtrusive silence of Japanese service, was incensed. There was, in fact, no use getting angry; the manageress was not insulting us, she was just trying to efficiently get the job done, get out of our way, and on to the next table.

THE MEALS OF THE DAY

Most Westerners, when thinking of Chinese cuisine, immediately think of rice, rice, rice. Indeed, in Mandarin and Taiwanese, the word *fan*, literally meaning 'rice', may be used to refer to meals and food in general. However, this may be a good time to point out that not all rice is equal. The rice consumed in Taiwan is the same as the Japanese Calrose variety—short-grained and sticky. It is better than the rice you will eat in Mainland China and different from the long-grained, fragrant rice favored by the Chinese from Thailand through to Singapore.

Breakfast

Taiwanese like to eat three 'squares' a day and then snack now and again. Breakfast is called *dzau tsan* (early meal) or *dzau fan* (early rice) and is normally taken between 7:00 and 9:00 a.m. If the family is Western-oriented, they might have a glass of milk with a slice of bread, into which has been folded either pork floss (*rou sz*) or a fried egg. Sometimes they might be prepared buns from the local bakery. These buns often have fillings that can be an annoying or pleasant 'surprise' for Westerners expecting a plain bun. It might be sweetened condensed milk, pork floss, tuna fish, sweetened bean paste, or a hotdog. If you aren't sure of the freshness, take care. This is especially true of some 'cream horns' or prepared sandwiches with mayonnaise. Think of your intestines before you purchase. Not to sound too loud a warning, we must also comment that we have had some excellent croissants and pastry from local Taiwanese bakeries as of late.

If the family prefers local taste, breakfast can be one of several things. Rice porridge (Mandarin *jou*, Taiwanese *buh*) is served with side dishes of peanuts, salted duck egg, pickled seaweed or cucumber, preserved fish, or canned fried gluten. Northern *Wai Sheng Ren* brought with them their *shau bing* and *you tyau* breakfast breads. *Shau bing* (roast cakes) are a flaky crusted bread pocket with sesame seeds sprinkled on the outside. *You tyau* (oil sticks) are deep-fried Chinese crullers. The chef will put a long thin string of dough into an immense oil-filled wok standing over a large flame. The string will balloon out to make a thin golden brown and crispy rod. This is folded in half and inserted in the *shau bing* pocket. It is frequently accompanied by *dou jyang* (soybean milk soup), which is served hot or cold, sweet or salty. The white sweet type is common and can be found everywhere. The hot salty type is made by taking raw soybean milk and adding a spoonful of dried pickled radish, sesame oil, chilli oil, salt, bits of broken *you tyau*, and shallots. It tastes like a divine cream of chicken soup. Worth looking for.

Lunch

For students, office workers, or factory people, lunch (*wu tsan* or *wu fan*, 'noon meal') is usually eaten between 12:00 and 1:00 p.m. and is frequently in a *byan dang* (lunch box). This term is not used in China and came from the Japanese *o bento*. The *byan dang* was traditionally brought from home and heated at the school or office. Today there are small eateries that sell them 'to-go' in styrofoam containers. They will also deliver to local offices.

Usually the meal contains steamed white rice and a fried pork chop, or fish, a chicken drumstick, or stewed pork, stir-fried vegetables, mustard greens, dried bean curd, etc. An alternative are the *dz ju tsan* (self-service meals) which are served in small cafeterias. In the late morning, the chefs will busy themselves cooking up vast aluminum trays of food: fried and steamed fish, eggplant, bean curd, greens, pork chops, fried eggs—usually 12 or more dishes. You are asked first if you want rice or porridge and then you can just point at what you want on top. The lady will heap it onto your disposable tray. A weak soup is also available.

Dinner

The ideal Taiwanese family will eat dinner together. The meal is called *wan fan* (late rice). They will usually have soup, two vegetables, and chicken or seafood—enough for a typical family of three. More dishes will be prepared if Grandma is around to help cook and eat. Today, though, Dad is out entertaining, Junior is off to cram school, so Mom eats a specialty at a push cart to remind her of the flavors of her youth.

When they have all returned home they might go out together for *syau ye* (midnight snack). This might be a bowl of noodles, or *chou doufu* (smelly bean curd—they say it smells like a sewer and tastes like a dream; bean curd's equivalent to Blue Stilton cheese). Or it could be *lu rou fan* (ground meat sauce on a bowl of rice), *rou geng* (breaded, deep-fried bits of meat in a thick sauce), or *rou dzung* (glutinous rice, egg, mushrooms, dried shrimp, and pork mixed together and steamed in a leaf).

Tomorrow, they have decided to go out for dinner. With so many hundreds of eateries and restaurants to choose from, the only problem is deciding where!

Just one of the many steet stalls which the Taiwanese frequent for their syau ye.

Regional Styles

The island's history as an entrepôt, the arrival of the two million *Wai Sheng Ren* from every corner of China in 1949, not to mention the bounty of local vegetables, fruit, and meat, all meant that Taiwan was destined to become a gastronomic paradise. A brief introduction to the regional cuisines is in order:

- **Taiwanese** (*Tai Tsai*). The cuisine of the local population is best known for its seafoods, pork, chicken, light soups, and use of crushed or sliced garlic. Look for stewed pig trotters (*ti pang*), clams fried with soy sauce and garlic (*hai gwa dz*), squid cooked with celery (*chye tsai hwa jr*), three-cup chicken (*san bei ji*), homemade-style bean curd (*jya chang doufu*), and omelette with preserved radish or oyster (*tsai pu jyan dan*).

- **Hakka** (*Kejya Tsai*). The Hakkas settled in Taiwan centuries ago and their cuisine is now very similar to the above. Specialties include stuffed bean curd (*niang doufu*), eggplant *basilico* (*jyou tseng ta chye dz*), and *teppanyaki* bean curd (*tyeban doufu*).
- **Sichuan** (*Chwan Tsai*) and **Hunan** (*Syang Tsai*). These cuisines from the south of central China both make liberal use of minced garlic and hot chillies. You can order the food to be prepared more mildly (*bu yau tai la*), but we have found this spicy food to be manageable by most of our foreign visitors. Look out for hot and sour soup (*swan la tang*), sauteed shrimp with hot sauce (*gan shau sya*), fish-flavored eggplant (*yu syang chye dz*), Ma Pwo bean curd (*Ma Pwo doufu*), 'bang bang' chicken (*bang bang ji*), camphor tea-smoked duck (*jang cha ya dz*), *kung pao* chicken (*gung bau jiding*), whole fish in hot bean sauce (*la dou ban yu*), dry cooked string beans (*gan byan sz ji dou*), and the famous numbing 'spicy fire pot' (*ma la hwo gwo*).
- **Cantonese** (*Au Tsai*). The Cantonese brought their style of cooking to the United States when they were used as forced labor on the railroads. Their cuisine became synonymous with Chinese food until the 1970s. However, it has been greatly damaged in the transition to the US and you should try this popular cuisine of southern China to get to know 'the real thing'. Cantonese cuisine occasionally uses heavier and thicker sauces, is milder than other Chinese food, and is very colorful. Some popular dishes are shrimp with cashew nuts (*yau gwo sya ren*), sweet and sour pork (*gu lau rou*), roast pork (*cha shau rou*), pork ribs with winter melon soup (*dung gwa pai gu tang*), abalone with Chinese broccoli and oyster sauce (*bau yu gai lan*).
- **Peking** (*Jing Tsai*). This is Mandarin cuisine from the north of

China. Look for more noodles and breads, and less rice. Famous dishes are Peking duck (*Beijing kau ya*), and rinsed mutton chafing dish (*shwan yang rou*)—a dish which is either cooked or kept warm at your table by means of a small, portable spirit stove.

• **Shanghai**. Cuisine from Shanghai and its surrounding areas features a lot of seafood and fish dishes. In particular, try Ningpo-style eel (*Ning Pwo shr shan yu*) and West Lake vinegar fish (*syi hu tsu yu*).

• **Vegetarian** (*Su Tsai*). China has some marvelous vegetarian cuisine, thanks to its Buddhist heritage. It tries to make vegetarianism for hard core omnivores a little easier to endure by making some dishes look and taste reasonably like meat—vegetarian goose (*su e*), for instance. Other popular dishes are fried gluten, hair vegetable stew (*fa tsai geng*), and vegetarian spring rolls (*su chwun jywan*).

• **Mongolian Barbecue** (*Menggu kau rou*). The concept of the barbecue is said to have evolved from the traveling kitchens of Genghis Khan's mounted forces. A large metal shield would be placed over a fire, game slaughtered, and local vegetables rounded up. Popular with both foreign visitors and locals, the barbecue in Taiwan is an all-you-can-eat buffet-style affair. Pick out your choice of raw meats, vegetables, and sauces, then watch the chef cook it before your eyes.

• **Steamboat** (*hwo gwo*). This is a cook-at-your-table, chafing dish. Pick out a selection of raw meats, seafoods, vegetables, *won ton*, and noodles. They will either be cooked in a stone pot (*shr tou hwo gwo*) or just a stainless steel pan at your table. Be sure to ask for Taiwan's famous *sha cha jiang* (literally 'sand tea paste'). It is a delicious, not too spicy sauce, into which Taiwanese will add a raw egg and maybe some soy sauce. Cooked food is then dipped into the mixture.

• *Dim Sum* (*dyan syin*). Normally associated with Cantonese cuisine, there are actually several regional *dyan syin* traditions. It is also known as *yin cha* (roughly meaning 'tea time'). Expect *dyan syin* only between 10:30 a.m. and 2:00 p.m. It is a boisterous substitute for lunch and comprises a variety of freshly cooked items served in round bamboo steamers. Waiters and waitresses will busily push carts loaded with these steamers to and fro through the aisles of the restaurant, where they are eagerly snapped up. Feel free to stop a waiter to ask to look at what he is selling. If you are not interested, just say, "No, thanks" (*sye sye, bu yau*), though you will find that it's all quite edible and delicious. Chosen items will be marked on a tally kept at your table. Popular *dyan sin* are steamed pork buns (*cha shau bao*), chicken claws (*feng jwa*), steamed pork ribs (*pai gu*), shrimp dumplings (*sya jyau*), and spring rolls (*chwun jywan*).

Regional Specialties

As you travel around Taiwan, it is worth noting that each area has its own local specialty foods to be eaten or taken back home as a souvenir. Although modern transport has made many of these items more universally available, they still make excellent gifts to give your Taiwanese and Western friends when you return home. They demonstrate *ren ching wei* (see Chapter Six) and can lead to discussions about Chinese food preparation and things you saw on your trip. The list below is by no means comprehensive and we hope you may make your own discoveries of other specialties!

- *Taiyang bing* (sun cakes). These are found in Taichung and are a flaky layered flat bun, white in color. In the center is a thin layer of sweet paste. They can be bought singly or by the box.
- *Dan dan myan* (noodles). This dish is a specialty of Tainan and is usually eaten at the stalls where it is cooked. It is made of yellow noodles, the size of spaghetti, which are cooked in a broth and then served with a crown of fragrant stewed ground pork. A dash of fresh coriander tops it off. Ask for a *lu dan* (Shandong egg) on the top. This is a very hard boiled egg that has been shelled and marinated or cooked in ground pork broth.
- *Ju swun gan* (dried bamboo shoots). These are found in Hsitou. Taken home, soaked, and stewed they make an excellent appetizer.
- *Wulung cha* (Oolong tea). The world's finest Oolong tea is grown

in Taiwan and the finest Taiwan Oolong is grown in Tungting.
- **Fresh apples and pears** from Lishan are particularly good.
- **Peanuts and peanut candy** are a specialty of Hsinchu.

The International

Although its has improved greatly through the years, the quality and variety of non-Chinese cuisine in Taiwan still leaves much to be desired. Fifteen years ago, a pizza comprised the bottom of a hamburger bun with a slice of spam, American cheese, and ketchup, toasted in a broiler. Now you will find many popular fast food chains from around the world. For quality Western dining, you might try one of the international hotels, but the meal will be very expensive and perhaps not as good as you might expect. Various pubs and restaurants claim 'expertise' in French, Swiss, or American cooking. The cuisines below, however, are well represented and come at affordable prices.

- **Japanese** (*Ri Ben Lyau Li*). Having been a colony of Japan for 50 years, the Taiwanese learned to cook and enjoy Japanese food. This, coupled with the booming trade and tourism links with Japan, means that authentic Japanese food is readily accessible. The Japanese names for some of the most popular styles are *sushi* (rice, seafood, and seaweed *hors d'oeuvres*), *sashimi* (raw seafood), *yakiniku* (barbecued meat on a stick), *teppanyaki* (meat and vegetables quickly grilled in front of you), *tempura* (seafood and vegetables, battered and deep-fried), and *udon* (thick noodles in a broth).
- **Thai, Indonesian, and Vietnamese**. Overseas Chinese from various areas have gone to Taiwan to set up eateries serving ethnic cuisine. The foods are refreshingly spicy and reasonably priced.

The Bizarre, the Macho, and the Illegal

Every nation has its strange and macho foods: prairie oysters (raw testicles) in the US, *balutte* (semi-incubated duck eggs) in the Philippines, *fugu* (the poisonous puffer fish) in Japan. Frequently, it is expected that their ingestion will improve one's sexual performance, or at least one's vitality. Translated into Taoist theory, such foods are very *yang* or create a lot of energy. Below are some foods which you may see on a menu or find being served to you during a 'night out with the guys'.

- **Sea Cucumber and Jellyfish.** Neither item is considered bizarre or macho by the Taiwanese. Sea cucumber is frequently served cooked in thick sauces, while jellyfish comes on cold platters. Sea cucumber is gelatinous and innocuous; it takes on the flavor of whatever it is cooked with. Jellyfish is usually served cold and shredded in a chilli, sesame, and vinaigrette seasoning. It has a chewy, rubbery consistency.
- **Whole Fish or Poultry**. Fish and poultry are frequently brought to the table in a state of wholeness that Westerners find shocking. That means cockscomb, head, eyes, brains, and feet (or fins). Of course, they have been gutted. Chris distinctly remembers the dinner he had, three weeks after arriving in Taiwan, when the lady of the house served up a boiled chicken, its head limply hanging over the rim of the pot, staring him straight in the eye. Superior flavor is the reasoning behind this custom. Feel honored if your host serves the meat from the fish's gill shield to you—it is reputed to be the most tasty.
- **Cracked Bones**. Chinese chefs, either before or after cooking, will cut a piece of chicken or pork clear through the bones. It is felt that greater flavor and nutrition is imparted to the dish this way and Taiwanese can frequently be seen gnawing on the marrow. However, this means that sometimes the dish can have sharp shards of bone in it, which you should be careful of. Bone pieces can be removed from your mouth with your chopsticks or spat onto your plate. Follow your friend's lead.
- **Braised Ox Phallus** or **Rooster and Tom Turkey Privates**. Enough said!
- **Snake's Blood Soup**. This is available mostly at Snake Alley, where vipers, cobras, and hundred-pacers (all very poisonous snakes)

are milked of venom, vivisected, and squeezed dry of blood and bile. This is often served as a cocktail, mixed with potent *gau liang* sorghum spirit. Alternatively, it can be boiled up as a soup with strips of snake meat.

• **Turtle's Blood Cocktails**. Again, these can be had at Snake Alley, or you could watch the movie *Farewell to My Concubine* to see how it's done. Turtles have long lives (well, not at Snake Alley!) and phallic-shaped heads, so they are presumed to be very *yang*. To make the cocktail, the head of the turtle is pulled out of the shell and chopped off. Then the shell is peeled back slightly (legs are still moving) and *gau liang* is poured into it, mixed, and then poured out with the blood. Bottoms up!

• **Dog Meat.** Called *syang rou* (fragrant meat) in Mandarin, it is actually illegal to sell it in Taiwan. Pets still disappear, though, and signs will occasionally appear on the street, saying 'Fragrant Meat for Sale'. Curiously, the Chinese view this as a 'heaty' tonic food to be consumed in winter, while the Koreans see it as a summer tonic. Whatever your belief, it certainly gives a new meaning to the song *How Much is that Doggy in the Window?*

A passer-by contemplates roasted sparrows on offer at a roadside stall.

- **Bear Paws**. It is said that when bears go into hibernation they store nutrients for the winter in their paw pads. Blissfully asleep, they lick the pads and are slowly fed. Consequently, the Chinese feel that, being so full of vitamins and minerals, bear pads make an excellent tonic. However, bears are endangered in China and, indeed, around the world. This is a very expensive dish and it is best to steer clear of it. If asked whether you will eat it, you might reply that your Chinese physician has told you only to eat eel as a tonic, not bear.
- **Betel Nut**. Though not typically thought of as a food, betel nut is best put in this section because it is chewed like a tobacco and sometimes referred to as 'Chinese chewing gum'. A betel nut is wrapped in a betel pepper leaf, after being smeared with an alkaline

paste. When chewed, the result is a blood-red mess in the mouth, which is frequently spat out onto the sidewalk and can be mistaken for rather nasty tubercular expectorations. (Now you know where the movie *Beetlejuice* got its name!) The effect of the juice is a mild narcotic high, which is nevertheless legal. Addicts can be readily picked out of the crowd by their stained teeth and bloody grin.

Tea Time

Tea drinking is a culture unto itself in Chinese societies and, in Taiwan, with its splendid Oolong, jasmine, chrysanthemum, and Tye Guan Yin varieties, this is so much the more so. It is interesting to note that, in all languages around the world, there are only two words for this beverage that originated in China, and both names are Chinese. *Cha* is the Mandarin name, which found its way into Japanese as *o cha*. *Teh* is the term in the Hokkien dialect, which of course found its way into English, French, and other languages.

There are many places where you might enjoy tea and the etiquette involved might vary. If you are invited to have tea or coffee during a business meeting, you might reply that you want 'Chinese tea'. If it is served to you in a Western teacup and there is no evidence of leaves, then it was brewed in a bag—no comment. If, however, it comes to you in a tall cup with a lid, it will probably have the leaves still seeping in hot water. The proper etiquette is to hold the cup in one hand and gently remove the lid with the other, holding it over the cup and sweeping the condensation from the tea back into the cup in a soft circular motion of lid against lip. Then, with the cup brought to the nose, lift the lid and smell the perfume of the tea. Finally, look at the surface of the water. Are there leaves still floating on the surface? If so wait a minute more. After that, repeat the process, but this time either gently blow the leaves away from the area you wish to drink from, or use the lid to push them out of the way.

Another privilege you may enjoy is to go to a teahouse or the house of a friend to enjoy *lau ren cha* (pensioner's tea), so called because old folk like to sit with friends, sipping, chatting, snacking, sipping, chatting, snacking, and so on. During *lau ren cha*, a small teapot, usually from Yisying (a town north of Shanghai which is famous for its teapots), is stuffed with tea leaves and placed in a small terracotta bowl in which tiny demi-tasse cups rest. Water which was boiled about 10 minutes before is poured into the pot, allowed to activate the leaves briefly, then poured *onto* the cups, ostensibly to rinse and heat them up. The cups are rolled around in the tea water, then removed with a pair of bamboo tweezers, and stood up in a row.

When the leaves have steeped, the tea is poured into the cups and your host will probably present your cup to you with some ceremony. Again, take the time to savor the aroma of the tea. There will be no leaves in it to blow away, so take a sip and roll it on your tongue. If you are drinking a quality Oolong, you may taste a slight bitterness behind the fragrance. After you have swallowed, however, you will most likely taste the sweetness of the saliva in your mouth. The Chinese believe this is good to swallow as it helps to build *chi*. The process of steeping and savoring is repeated as often as 10 or 12 times for a quality tea, the taste varying to the connoisseur's palate each time round. In between, snacks designed not to interfere with either the enjoyment of the tea or the meandering of the conversation, are enjoyed.

It is enjoyable and worthwhile acquainting yourself with Chinese teas. They are a source of pride to the Taiwanese, can provide plenty of opportunity to break the ice and get to know people, and may become a lifelong obsession for you as well.

DINING OUT
The Invitation

Invitations from Taiwanese are normally warm, sincere, and spur-of-the-moment. Do not expect a week's notice for an informal dinner. You might be on the phone with a Taiwanese friend at 3:00 p.m. and be asked out to dinner that night. Let's say you are free and want to go. Return the warmth and sincerity of the invitation in your words and voice. For example, "That sounds great. I have never been to that restaurant before. Thank you." Make sure you get the time and place properly noted. If there is any question, ask to be met at a more obvious popular landmark.

If you are not free, do not just say,"No, thank you". This does not show *ren ching wei*. You should preferably have a reason for not going that is bigger than the face of the person asking. That way, he or she does not lose face. This is especially important if the invitation is given in person in front of a group. For example, you are invited to dinner with a business associate, but have another business dinner planned. If you just say ,"I'm sorry, but I have a dinner planned with Mr. Y of company Z," it may chill relations. You may not know the inviter's relation or relative status to Mr. Y. What you are saying indirectly is, "He is more important than you." Better to say something like, "I wish I could come, but I have bought tickets for my daughter's play/have to be at the school to give a test to students/have to wait at the hotel for a long conference call with my boss."

Since many invitations are spur-of-the-moment, it is not appropriate to add, "But can we go next week?" if you must decline. Better to say ,"But I have left Monday night open and planned to invite you and your staff to dinner." Your invitation will probably be turned down, but it leaves the door open.

Note that, because of the sincere persistence required of *ren ching wei*, some excuses will not do. For instance, you are invited to play a round of golf, a game you have admitted to having played before. If you refuse, using the excuse that you don't have your shoes, they will say, "We can rent shoes at the clubhouse." To say you do not want to wear rented shoes is too stuffy. If you say 'no' because you do not have a handicap yet, they will say, "No matter, we can fix it up with the club to let you play." You really must think of a good reason not to take up the invitation.

Invitations to weddings, *man ywe*, *man swei*, and company New

Year's banquets will be issued in writing or in advance. A wedding banquet (*syi jyou*) invitation is normally red with gold lettering. Invitations to company banquets, on the other hand, will usually be relayed by word of mouth.

The Casual Meal

A typical casual business lunch is described in Chapter Nine. Expect the same situation in any Chinese restaurant which is a step above the cafeterias. Ordering is usually done off the menu. If you are with Taiwanese, avoid the temptation to order for the group. Unless you have been in Taiwan for a long time and know the specialties of the restaurant's regional cuisine, then you should ask your Taiwanese friends to order, even if (perhaps *especially* if) you are the host. Out of courtesy, they may ask you to order. Politely insist that *they* order. Do not even peruse the menu; this implies you want to have some say. Turn it over to the 'big shot' at the table.

Why? Invariably they will know the house specialty (*jau pai tsai*). They also know the quantities and proper mix to order. Letting them select gives them face, it says you trust them, and, if you are the host, it lets them order things they will enjoy. It also saves you the embarrassing problem of having ordered too little or too many 'cheap' dishes. So far, our Taiwanese friends have not abused this trust by ordering only the most expensive things and, moreover, it reaps more *ren ching wei* points.

When you insist they order, you should advise them that you do not like, for instance, sweet and sour pork or cream of *sum yung gai* (yes, it's a joke alright!) because otherwise they may order according to what they *think* a foreigner's taste is. But you should ask them specifically not to order a certain dish, only if you really can't handle it (that means you are allergic to it!). Who knows, maybe this restaurant has a tastier way of preparing *hai je* (sea cucumber)? It is completely appropriate to ask what they have ordered and to review the dishes one by one as they come. Individual dishes frequently have stories behind them and this can become one of the most interesting things about the repast. It also lets you prepare for what kind of food will be set before you.

How do Taiwanese order foods? They will normally order one dish per person, plus a soup and rice or noodles. If the meal is for four people, they might order, for example, one meat, one fish, two vegetable dishes, one soup, and plain white rice. Certain styles or types of dishes are not repeated. For instance, two sweet and sour dishes, or two shrimp dishes will not be ordered together. Unlike in the West, Taiwanese do not order for individual diners. This goes back to the practice of the family always eating together as a group. Unless you are eating lunch box-style, the dishes are almost invariably shared.

You will be expected to try everything. Respond enthusiastically to dishes which you like and give a reasoned explanation of why. Likewise, politely say that the things you do not like are not to your taste, but be sure you have tried some first. Anyway, they will know what you do not enjoy by watching you, so it is best to be upfront.

Mind Your Manners

During the meal it is possible that the host or your neighbor will serve your plate. He or she will do this either with the serving spoon or 'public-use' chopsticks (*gung yung kwaidz*), which should be returned to the dish they came from. Alternatively, they might deftly reverse their own chopsticks and use the back end. Thank them for their hospitality. Though it is not expected, you may return the gesture with another dish later, but make sure you use the public-use chopsticks and return them to the platter afterward. If you aren't so deft at using chopsticks, it is probably best to sit this one out, rather than risk dropping food over your host (it has happened!).

When serving yourself, you should again use the public-use chopsticks or serving spoon, if provided. If they are not provided, you may ask for public-use chopsticks to be brought to the table. Your friends will not think this queer and may possibly commend you on your knowledge of Taiwanese eating habits. If it is a very informal group of friends, and they are using their own chopsticks to serve themselves, then you may do so. However, do not dredge your chopsticks or spoon through the food looking for a choice morsel. Do not even reach across to the opposite side of the plate to get that nice-looking shrimp. It is considered selfish and greedy. Select a piece near to your side of the plate and go for it.

Chopsticks should not be used as drumsticks to bang or tap the table with; nor should you plant them in your serving of rice so that they stand up. This reminds Taiwanese of incense sticks in a censer, used when praying for the dead, so it is not a good sign at the table.

Depending on the class of company you keep, loud belching could be considered rude, acceptable, or naturally expected. Taiwanese are uninhibited at times and belches are frequently heard in mid-sentence: "Hey, Chris, did you—belch—go to Taichung yesterday?" No apology proffered or expected.

Toothpicks will either be on the table or brought to it at the end of the repast, sometimes stuck in pieces of fruit. The Chinese like picking their teeth, be it for hygiene or to get full value from the meal. However, do not open your yap and dig in; the Taiwanese do not want to see your tonsils. In fact, they usually cover the mouth with the left hand, while industriously mining away with the right.

The Fight for the Check

Even if you were the one to invite your Taiwanese friends or colleagues out to dinner, drinks, karaoke, and the rest of it, expect a fight for the check. This is not a fight because nobody wants to pay, but the fight of who has the *privilege* to pay. Frequently you will see perfectly happy diners suddenly erupt into a flurry of emotion and hand-waving. You wait for them to come to blows as the volume increases. Don't be alarmed. This is merely proper gamesmanship. If it was clearly your invitation to them, make sure you win. Do not let them pull the tab out of your hands and just say, "Okay, thanks." If they have invited you, make a show of trying to get the tab, but eventually yield it to the host, otherwise he loses face.

Sometimes the fight for the check begins at the time of the invitation. The scenario may go something like this. You invite several friends out to dinner. They have already treated you before. One of them insists that he invite you. The frequent ruse given is, "This is my country. When I come to visit your country, you can invite me out." The best reply to this is to jovially (never brusquely) insist that: a) they treated you last time; b) you have been in Taiwan for a while and this is now your second home; and c) without question, you expect them to visit when they come to your country and let you treat them, so this is just your pleasure to take them out now.

One strategy to ensure that you win the fight for the check (if it is known to be your treat) is to discreetly leave your credit card with the cashier before or during the dinner. The same blizzard of grabbing hands will fly when the bill comes, but they will realize at a glance that it is too late, and have to commend you on your artifice. Express your gratitude that they accompanied you for the meal.

Banquets

You know from Chapter Six what kinds of gifts to bring to certain types of banquet celebrations. If it is a banquet in your honor, or just a large group of diners joining together for a good meal, you might consider bringing a gift. A bottle of whiskey (Johnnie Walker preferably) is reasonable and may well be opened at the banquet to be enjoyed by all. Give it to the host, though.

The banquet table is always round and seats 10 to 12 people. Expect to find it in an individual room for your party. The guest of honor will sit to the right of the host in a chair which faces the door and has its back to a wall. This harks back to Chinese chivalric courtesy: the safest and therefore most honored seat was the one with no entry behind you and a view of your enemies ahead. If you are not

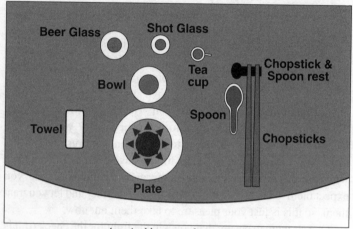

A typical banquet place-setting.

sure if you are the guest of honor, wait to be shown to your seat.

At each place-setting, expect to find:

- a soup bowl
- a small plate
- a chopstick-rest and spoon-rest
- chopsticks (sometimes the wrapped, sanitary type)
- a metal serving spoon
- a ceramic soup spoon
- a napkin or cold face towel
- a teacup
- a shot glass
- a juice/beer glass

The table usually has a tablecloth and a 'lazy Susan' at its center. The lazy Susan (a small revolving platform at the center of the table) rotates either way to give you access to the many dishes that will be delivered. Do not play with it or spin it too fast. When you arrive, it may already have some *syau chr* (little snacks) on it, such as peanuts or dried watermelon seeds. Follow the lead of the Taiwanese to gauge when you can begin to eat these. You may have to wait for the guest of honor, host, or other big shot to arrive. He or she may be late. Spend the time chatting with your friends and asking them the rules of banqueting. Unless the person is extraordinarily late or you hear the Taiwanese complaining, it is best not to comment on punctuality.

When the guest of honor has arrived, the first course—normally an assorted cold plate—will be brought to the table. In some restaurants, a waitress will serve a helping of each course onto individual plates or bowls. At other places, you serve yourself. Go with the flow. In all, 10 or 12 dishes and soups may be served. Pace yourself. Try not to 'chow down' the first two courses because you are hungry, only to end up wishing you had room to squeeze in a taste of the last three courses.

The last main course (and it is a signal that things are slowing down) is usually a rice, fried rice, or noodle dish. Other culture guides to Taiwan state that you should not eat this at all. We have not found that to be true. You will see the Taiwanese eating it. However, it is considered bad form to finish your helping or, especially, to ask for more, no matter how good it tastes. To do so signifies you are still hungry, that the host was terribly remiss in not ordering enough, and that you are going home unsated. Shame on your host!

After rice, a plate of fresh fruit will normally be served. At some northern-style Chinese banquets either a sweet steamed rice and preserved fruit dish (*ba bau fan*), or crepes with sweet bean paste filling might be served. Other than this, do not expect or ask for dessert.

If you are the guest of honor, it is important to know when to leave, as they will be waiting for you to make a sign. No more than 15 to 20 minutes should pass after the last course and fruit is brought out. You should then thank the host profusely for the bounty they has provided, for the thoughtful attention they showed in ordering such delicious foods, and for the friendship shown during all the toasting. If things are going well and you are so inclined, it would not hurt to invite the host out for further partying at a bar or karaoke lounge, but not for a snack, cake, or other food.

Banquet Drinking

Depending on the function of the banquet, different types of toasting will take place. At family milestone banquets (weddings, *man ywe*, *man swei*), the hosts will go to each table to toast a glass. Usually this is beer or *shao sying jyou* (amber-colored Chinese rice wine served warm or at room temperature, frequently with rock sugar or a dried plum in the glass). At a company function, the boss will toast each table. Toasting will also take place among the guests at each table. Indeed, it is considered poor form to take a drink of alcohol (or any drink besides tea) without it being a toast. The man across the table from you may raise his glass to you. He is honoring you. He is also thirsty. It would be unthinkable not to salute him with your glass. The usual toasting salutation is a boisterous *gan bei!* which has the same characters as the Japanese *kam pai*, meaning 'dry glass'. At some time during the dinner, the toast should be returned. Just think of it: nine people toasting you, plus nine returns make 18 glasses of beer or shots of wine. And we haven't even counted the people from other tables in the banquet who may come over especially to toast the foreigner!

The Taiwanese, especially men, like to drink and think they are good at it. Indeed, they generally hold their liquor better than Japanese, but have the same genetic tendency to turn red in the face with their first beer. They like drinking with foreigners, are eager to introduce you to the local spirits, and appreciate a good drinker. Some women drink moderately, but those who can 'put it away with the best of them' are generally considered 'bad' (i.e. morally loose or even a prostitute). This attitude is changing among college-age girls, but as they age, they still do not want to be associated with 'darker elements'. Foreign women who can drink heavily will be held to a different standard than local women and might be an amusing fascination to the other dinner guests. The impression left is risky though. Temperance is advised.

Temperance Strategies

For the person who does not want to drink alcohol, there are several alternatives, depending on the function. If you never drink because of religion or health, just say so. Juice is available to toast with. This excuse means they should not find you with beer in hand next week. Alternatively, if you are driving, you can try the 'designated driver' excuse; explain what it means in the West, and hope they do not think you too much of a wimp. If you can take a little alcohol, but not too much, do not drain your glass with every toast. The person who toasted you will point it out, but you can smile and laugh it off, and they will understand.

At one banquet (a source of fond memories for Chris and his Taiwanese host), the host announced to the group that he knew Chris did not like to drink too much, so he had brought him a special glass. He popped the tiniest of shot glasses on the table top. He continued amid laughter, "And I have chosen a special plum for his glass." He then put the largest of dried plums inside. There was hardly any room left for wine! You might try a similar strategy.

We also know a high-powered American executive who brings with him to banquets his own 'designated drinker' (a company employee who takes the successive belts for him). For heavy duty banqueting this might give him tremendous status, but he does not get any of the face from being able to loosen his tie and commune with the locals in their most relaxed state. He admits, too, that even with the designated drinker, he occasionally gets roped into drinking bouts.

A final note about banquets: there is never any question about who picks up the tab and hence no fighting for the bill!

–Chapter Eight–

ENJOYING TAIWAN

Whether you have come to Taiwan on holiday or to live and work, you should try to get to know the people. The more you travel around the island, the more you introduce yourself to the regional cuisines and appreciate the many and varied outings and holidays that you can have, the more you will have a chance to interact directly with the friendly people here. There is so much to do, see, eat, and enjoy that no time need be spent lonely or unoccupied.

Taiwanese work hard all day: night-time is when they play. As with dining, Taiwanese entertainment revolves around *re nau* (literally, 'hot and raucous', but a term generally indicative of lively and noisy activity). Everywhere is *re nau*: on the streets the hawkers selling clothes, sausages, fruit, teapots; the roar of hundreds of motorcycles; the endless shop signs setting the evening alight. Similarly, the Taiwanese like their movie entertainment to be *re nau*: kung fu movies, Rambo, Schwarzeneggar, slapstick. In the movie theater, don't be surprised if the couple sitting next to you are noisily enjoying fried chicken or leathery dried squid, or if rather loud laughing and chattering are going on. The audience are simply enjoying themselves as well as the movie!

Perhaps this kind of behavior dates back to the spectacular Chinese opera shows in 1920s China. Half the spectacle was actually in the audience, as pastries, tea, and hot towels were delivered and consumed during the performance, the towels being thrown through the air, back to the towel boy.

Most religious observances are also *re nau*. *Re nau* is pageantry and spectacle, color and emotion, the noise of large gatherings of people enjoying themselves. "Why can't we just take a little quiet respite from the noise of this life here?" a tired Westerner laments. But you must remember, for the Taiwanese, respite from the noise in this life is death. They are in no hurry. Try to enjoy life with them, their way, especially if they invite you to do so.

BESIDES EATING

Though you may get the impression from all the full restaurants you see around you that the only entertainment in Taiwan is eating, you would be missing out on half of what goes on.

Cinema

Movies are popular in Taiwan. Western films are usually in English with Chinese subtitles. A European movie, however, might be in the original language without English subtitles, so beware. Chinese movies normally have both Chinese and English subtitles.

Chinese films fall into several categories: serious dramas of high quality (these are rare); action movies (which include police, soldier, military chivalric, and kung fu themes); banal comedies; and 'cry me a river' tear-jerking family dramas. Hardcore pornography is not screened publicly.

Movie theaters are spread around the city now. The Times Square of Taipei is Syi Men Ding (the Point of the Western Gate), where 10 or so theaters and several department stores are clustered within 10 minutes' walk of each other. Also like Times Square, this part of town has a reputation for low-life, prostitution, and drugs. Beware.

Movie tickets can only be bought one hour in advance of the show time. At the right time, a curtain will open at the ticket window and the attendant will let you choose which seats you want. Each person is only allowed to buy a maximum of four tickets per visit to the window. So, if you have a large group or family, make sure enough people stand in line to buy the required number of tickets.

This ticketing arrangement creates its own problems. When blockbuster movies hit town, the ticket scalpers (low-life, all) emerge from the woodwork. In Mandarin they are called *hwang nyou* (yellow cows). A clique of them wait in line for every show. Though the ticket line may extend around the block, somehow the regular folk near the front merely complain, but otherwise tolerate the shenanigans of the *hwang nyou* who continually break back into line with their cronies. When the ticket window curtain is closed, all the seats sold out, the *hwang nyou* disperse through the disappointed crowd selling their tickets with a 50–100 percent mark-up. It is not wise to argue with them; they are a group and are sometimes lightly armed. Try to find a policeman instead.

Did you manage to get a ticket? If you did, you will notice that the theater seats are divided left and right into *dan hau* (odd numbers) and *shwang hau* (even numbers) respectively. Before the movie starts there will be some commercials for things like juice, motor scooters, or life insurance, along with some movie previews if you are lucky. Then the national anthem of the Republic of China will be played with a short film clip. Everyone is expected to rise, stand to quiet attention and stop eating. That means you, too. At the end, everyone sits down and the movie begins. Lastly, try to look around the theater before the lights go down and make sure you know where the emergency exit (*tai ping men*) is located. Note that smoking is not allowed in the theater, so if the guy next to you lights up, feel free to point out the sign to him.

MTV

In Taiwan, this does not stand for Music Television. Rather, it is a new industry unto itself: Movie Television. Remember, in Taiwan, extended familes prevail. A high school- or college-age son usually has no car and there is no history of the drive-in movie in Taiwan, so he can't go 'parking' with his girlfriend. The house is never empty. So what's a boy to do if he wants to make out? Enter MTV. For about US$8, he and his girlfriend can sit on a couch in their own dark, air-conditioned, private cubicle and watch the movie of their choice. This may even be a *hwang se* (a 'yellow' one, as opposed to the 'blue' ones in the West), which means it will be sexy. There are already over 1,000 MTV's operating on the island, many for 24 hours a day.

KTV

This stands for Karaoke Television. 'Karaoke', you may well know, is a Japanese term that literally means 'empty orchestra'. It is an advanced sing-along system. In Taiwan you will frequently see signs for KTV and you can take your family, friends, or business associates along. You can get a private room, have snacks served up, and order songs to croon to in the relative privacy of your own sound-proof room. The lyrics will appear on the screen, along with a video to go with the music. English, Mandarin, Taiwanese, and Japanese songs are normally stocked. Check the charges per song and for snacks before you take the room, otherwise you might be in for a big ($$$)

surprise at the end of the evening!

More recently some KTV joints have begun to overlap into hostess bars, so check the place out before you bring the kids. There are also karaoke pubs which are basically bars with a karaoke rig, except here you sing to a crowd of inebriated strangers. The choice is yours!

Light Gambling

Although illegal in Taiwan, certain forms of gambling are ignored. *Mahjong* is an example. This is similar to a Western card game, but is played with tiles instead of cards. There is a whole culture of gambling etiquette established around *mahjong* and many movies in recent years have glorified the prowess of mystic *mahjong* gambling kings. The Chinese will bet considerable amounts of money on *mahjong* and some sit up until the small hours playing this addictive game. You may see it being played or hear the clacking sound of the tiles being shuffled on the table as you walk by windows, or down side streets.

Try your luck at pachinko *(pinball) and win a juicy sausage, but don't count on getting a free dinner this way; Chris has never won a sausage yet!*

Pachinko is a Japanese game usually compared to pinball. In Japan it is controlled by the underworld and is a mild form of gambling. The cabinets stand vertically and the player shoots small ball bearings up and through a maze of pins. Credit (in the form of more balls) is given, depending on which hole the balls eventually drop through. At the end of the session, the player turns in his remaining balls (hopefully more than he or she started out with) to the collection window where they can get a prize. The bright lights, noise, and monotony make this game *re nau* in a mind-numbing way.

Recent years have seen the rise of an underground lottery system called *Da Jya Le* (Everybody's Happy). On a monthly basis, bets would be placed on certain numbers and there are many stories of factory workers retiring on their winnings. However, the lottery was a racket that disrupted factory and office productivity, and it has now been stepped on by the government.

Instead, the government runs its own ingenious numbers lottery that has a very distinct and practical purpose. Like business people the world over, Taiwanese are averse to surrendering their tax dollars to the powers that be. Businessmen often kept two sets of accounts for their enterprises: one set that deflated earnings and one that showed the real situation. Then the government instituted the Unified Invoice System (*Tung Yi Fa Pyau*). On a monthly basis, all businesses must purchase a booklet of these numbered invoices from the taxman. The populace is encouraged to ask for their receipts when making purchases as a monthly grand prize draw is made with the invoice numbers. The winning numbers are posted in the newspaper. Ask your secretary to help you keep track if you want to win.

On some streets in Taiwan you may also see an old man with charcoal brazier and a home-made *pachinko* board on the back of his bike. Cooking on the grill are nice, fat, juicy Taiwanese sausages. Try your luck—probably about NT$10 per try. Chris has not won a sausage yet and has always ended up asking the man to sell him one!

For Culture Vultures

Cultural entertainment of some sort takes place every week in Taiwan. Several excellent ballet troupes perform original and classical works. Try, in particular, to see the Cloud Gate Ensemble while you are in Taiwan.

Traditional opera of several regional varieties is also performed. It used to be that, during festivals, a stage would be erected in the middle of a back street for several days so that *ge dzai syi* (Hokkien opera) and *bu dai syi* (puppet shows) could be performed. You may still see that occasionally, but more often a screen is draped over a line across the road and films projected onto it for the whole neighborhood to see. Beijing opera (*Ping jyu* or *Jing jyu*) is performed in theatres. Do not count on being able to understand the words, but the music, color, acrobatics, and action are sufficiently stimulating.

With increasing frequency, big name pop acts are stopping in Taiwan. Listen to ICRT (the local English language radio station) for details. Tickets are expensive and sell fast.

A stall selling some of the beautiful puppets used in traditional street shows.

FESTIVALS AND HOLIDAYS

We have already stressed the Taiwanese love of *re nau* and this is nowhere more clearly seen than during festivals and holidays. The various festival celebrations that occur during the year allow them to stretch into ever louder and more raucous celebrations. Festivities and holidays revolve either around those that are religious or cultural, or those that are political and governmental. The dates of the former are determined by the farmer's calendar (the lunar *nungli*) and the latter are determined by the solar (Western) calendar. Here they are discussed in the order in which they fall in the solar calendar.

Founding Day of the Republic of China

Conveniently celebrated on New Year's Day (of the solar calendar), this holiday commemorates the founding of the Republic of China on January 1, 1912, following the overthrow of the Qing Dynasty.

Chinese New Year

Also called *Chwun Jye* (Spring Festival), parts of this celebration occur over a six-week period, from the eighth day of the last month of the farmer's calendar to the 15th day of the first month. Chinese New Year's Day will normally fall between January 10 and February 19. It is the grandest holiday for all Chinese around the world and is celebrated in many ways during the course of the season, depending on your age, sex, and marital status. It celebrates the birth of a new year, a time for renewed hope, the coming of spring, and fresh crops. Three days of official holiday are given around the change of the year. Depending on how outgoing you are and whether or not you have Taiwanese friends, it will be either a splendid and culturally enriching time or your loneliest three days spent in Taiwan.

Prior to New Year's Eve, businesses and individuals will feverishly crisscross the city settling old accounts. It is considered bad luck to have debts and accounts due when the New Year arrives. Pawnbrokers do a bumper business as people try to turn assets into paper money for the purpose of renewing credit. It is important, too, for businesses and individuals to collect what is owed them, for expenses peak during the New Year.

A business will normally have a banquet for its employees at this time. The cost can run into the tens of thousands of dollars for a medium-sized enterprise At the banquet, there will normally be some sort of prize draw. The prizes are subsidized by the business, donated by the owners, or contributed by major suppliers. If your company is asked to contribute a gift to another company's banquet, figure on spending a minimum of NT$3,000–10,000. Cameras, household appliances, and gift certificates are appropriate. Employees also expect to receive a New Year bonus. This amounts to a minimum of one month's extra salary, or more if the company is doing well. Some companies will plan company trips before or after New Year as another employee perk. Even a medium-sized enterprise might book a trip for all its employees to go to Bangkok, Hong Kong, or at least Kenting.

The individual also has increased expenses. On New Year's Eve the whole family will gather for a sumptuous dinner at home. Unmarried children receive *hung bau* (See Chapter Six, *Gift Giving*) with *ya swei chyan* (literally, 'push the year money') inside them. The children will visit relatives in their homes, run up to them, and politely demand, "*Gung Syi Fa Tsai! Hung bau na lai!*" (Congratulations and Be Prosperous! Hand over the red envelope!).

When visiting Taiwanese friends during the holiday, you should keep a pocketful of *hung bau*. Put one bright red NT$100 note in each so you are ready in case the children come to you. If they are too shy to come forward, it is very *ren ching wei* to ask them, "Aren't you going to ask for your *hung bau*?" It is also good manners to bring baskets of fruit, especially mandarin oranges, for they look like gold and are consumed by merrymakers during the 24-hour snacking that takes place.

Inside homes and offices, you might see black or gold Chinese characters painted on red paper and pasted to the walls and doors. If you are really astute, you will see the character *chwun* 春 (springtime) pasted upside down on the wall. This is because the phrase 'Spring turned upside down' has a similar sound in Chinese to 'Spring has arrived'. You will also see images of fish, especially goldfish, everywhere. This is because the word 'fish' (*yu*) sounds like the word 'surplus' (*yu*)—in other words, prosperity. Many New Year greetings revolve around this twist of words.

At midnight on New Year's Eve, the staccato thunder of dozens of strings of exploding firecrackers can be heard across the city. Your sleep will be intermittently interrupted until about 3:00 a.m. by this noise, designed to welcome the new year and scare evil away.

On the first day of New Year, it is appropriate to have new clothes ready for everyone in the family to wear. The day is spent visiting relatives, seeing movies, snacking, gambling, and playing *mahjong*. Even children join in on the betting, as older siblings try (often successfully) to win *ya swei chyan* from the younger ones in games of dice-in-a-bowl and poker. The clickety-clack of shuffling *mahjong* tiles can be heard coming from second-story windows everywhere.

On the second day of New Year, it is customary to allow one's wife to visit her family. In decades gone by, the wife became the virtual property of the husband, as well as fair game for ill-treatment from her mother-in-law, whose viciousness is legendary in Chinese culture. But at New Year, the wife was freed to go back to her family for a day. The plight of the modern Taiwanese housewife is not quite so bad these days, but the custom persists.

You might decide to join the crowd of thousands who want to see one of the blockbuster movies released at New Year (the equivalent of Hollywood's Christmas releases). Be aware that pickpockets and *hwang nyou* are working overtime during the festive season and will be in line with you (see *Cinema* above).

On the third day of New Year, it is considered better luck to stay indoors. Morning, noon, and night the television stations will be broadcasting New Year specials, none of them very much different from the other, nor from last year's offerings. You will be inundated with choruses of *Gung Syi, Gung Syi, Gung Syi Ni Ah!* (Congrats, Congrats, Congrats To You!), until you will feel like screaming. Before you do scream, just remember that any Taiwanese visiting, for example, the U.S. during Christmas time will be buried under drifts of Bing Crosby's *White Christmas* and the like.

During the holiday break, the opening of stores, restaurants, and other businesses is at the option of the owner. Many small shops might take up to two weeks off, so don't get caught with an empty fridge or with all your laundry at the dry cleaners'! Ask in advance if the shops you regularly patronize will be taking time off. Convenience stores, cinemas, and many department stores may stay open, but banks and government services are definitely off for the three days. Wet market food prices go up 15–25 percent as the stall holders dig deeper into everyone's purses for New Year cheer. Taxis become more scarce and may demand a quoted fare rather than a metered one. If you decide to leave Taipei or Taiwan altogether for a break, you will not be alone. Book *way* in advance; six months beforehand is not too soon. You may also be asked to pay a peak season premium at many regional resorts.

Lantern Festival

This marks the last day of the New Year Festival and comes two weeks after New Year's Eve, on the 15th day of the new moon. In old China, this was a magical day, the only day when virtuous young maidens were allowed to go out alone into the evening carrying beautiful delicate paper lanterns, there to be espied by prospective suitors under the golden glow of the candle light. Today, it is just another part of New Year and is celebrated by youngsters of both sexes, carrying plastic battery-powered lamps in many shapes. Traditional lantern contests are still held at the Lung Shan Temple and Guandu Temple.

Youth Day and Women's Day

Women's Day is on March 8. Celebrated in the Republic since 1924, on Women's Day female employees in the government and in some businesses will be allowed a day off. (It is also interesting to note here that the words *san ba* [three, eight] corresponding to March 8, is also used to describe 'ditzy' or 'scatterbrained' women!)

Youth Day falls on March 29. It is not a bank holiday, but children will get a day off school and may get to go on outings or do special activities with their school or with the clubs and societies to which they belong.

Tomb Sweeping Day and the Anniversary of Chiang Kai Shek's Death

March 5 is also a holiday to observe the death of Chiang Kai Shek. This coincides with the Tomb Sweeping Festival.

In Chapter Six, under the section on funerals, we commented on the expense and trouble the Taiwanese go to in order to find a proper and auspicious burial place for their relatives. Chinese cemeteries are not managed the way they are in the West, with a yearly upkeep fee and hired gardeners. Most tombs are left to go to seed with tall grass and weeds during the year. But in the West, the graves are rarely revisited by the whole family. In Taiwan, it is a yearly ritual to hike out into the mountains, following the lonely path that leads through tall grass and hundreds of other tombs, to find the one belonging to your relative. Once there, the family set it right by cleaning, sweeping, cutting down the grass, burning incense before an offering of food, and burning paper money in the small chimney built into the tomb.

Beigang Matsu Festival

Held once a year on the goddess Matsu's birthday (April/May of the lunar calendar) at her principal temple in Beigang (four hours' drive south of Taipei), this festival is a sight not to be missed. Teams of devotees from all over the island bear their local gods on palanquins

191

(enclosed litters borne on the shoulders) to participate in the celebration of the birthday of their liege. This amounts to literally hundreds of palanquins. As they approach the temple they set off string after string of firecrackers to scare evil spirits from their path. A blue-gray haze fills the air as you wade ankle-deep through the paper of spent firecrackers. Mountains of spirit money and forests of incense are burned. At night, you can see *dangki* (trance mediums) go into trances and flagellate themselves with swords and nail-encrusted wooden rods.

Devotees bearing their local god on a palanquin pause to let off firecrackers during the Matsu festival.

The Dragon Boat Festival

Celebration of this festival during the month of June includes perhaps the only sporting event in the world to have been inspired by a drowning bureaucrat. In 221 B.C. the famous poet-scholar and counsellor, Chu Yuan, began to advocate a policy of resistance to the unpopular emperor Chin. He found his opinions spurned and rival courtiers began to plot against him. In protest, he drowned himself.

The people were so taken by his expression of loyalty to his principles that they threw *dzung dz* (rice dumplings) into the lake so the fish would feed on them rather than the patriot's body.

Today the festival is celebrated with the famous Dragon Boat Races that can be watched in many countries where Chinese have settled. They symbolize the attempted rescue of Chu Yuan. In Taiwan, this has become quite an organized event, with teams coming from as far away as Australia and the U.S. to compete in eliminations and final rounds. Rice dumplings are also eaten at this time.

Ghost Month

Traditional beliefs indicate that on the first day of the seventh lunar month, the Gates of Hell open and allow the spirits condemned to the netherworld a chance for a break. In Chapter Five, we explained the

During Ghost Month the table is set for ghostly ancestors to eat their fill.

193

influence that spirits have over the world of the living, the importance of appeasing them and keeping them properly fed and financed. Particularly cautious Chinese will be very careful in their undertakings during this month: weddings are not held, new business not started, and so forth. On the 15th day of the month, a feast is prepared for the ghosts at home. The table is set and dishes brought out on the lazy Susan. Then incense and paper money are burned. After waiting for an appropriate time, to let the ghosts have their fill, the family sits down to enjoy the 'leftovers'.

Confucius' Birthday

The celebrated scholar-philosopher's birthday is remembered on September 28. At Confucian temples, special and very solemn rites are held in traditional costume and with traditional music. Tickets are available for you to attend, but must be arranged way in advance.

Mid-Autumn Festival

The vast majority of Chinese have tradionally been farmers. The Harvest Moon Festival, as it is known in the West, is also celebrated in Chinese tradition at the happy end of a period of summer sowing and reaping. The actual day of celebration falls on the 15th day of the eighth lunar month. By this time the grain would have been traditionally dried and stored, and all things would be ready for the winter. It was a time of rejoicing before the long, cold months arrived, the last festivities before the coming of the new year in spring.

Today the Mid-Autumn Festival is celebrated by families going out to view the full moon, drink Chinese tea, and eat mooncakes—small, round, rich cakes filled with a variety of sweet pastes, nuts, and egg yolks. Firecrackers and sparklers are also popular with the children.

National Day and 'Political' Celebrations

National Day falls on October 10, hence it is also known as 'Double Ten' Day. It is a public holiday in Taiwan and commemorates the fall of the Qing Dynasty, which led to the establishment of the Republic of China. Grand parades with marching bands, floats, and military hardware are reviewed by the president in front of the presidential building downtown.

Other public holidays in a similar vein to National Day, which fall toward the end of the year, include:

- Retrocession Day (October 25). A public holiday which marks the day Taiwan was returned by Japan to Chinese sovereignty.
- Chiang Kai Shek's Birthday (October 31). Another public holiday in honor of the Kuomintang leader.
- Sun Yat Sen's Birthday (November 12). A public holiday which commemorates the birth of China's equivalent to George Washington.
- Constitution Day (December 25). A holiday which happily, but not coincidentally, falls on Christmas Day.

THE SIGHTS AND MUST-SEES OF THE ILHA FORMOSA

Taipei has much to be explored in itself. There are several good guide books listed in the Bibliography at the back of this book which will be of help in planning your excursions. Here, we will point out things you really should endeavor to see in order to enrich your understanding of Taiwan, but we will leave other guides to give you the details.

Lung Shan Temple Area

This is a very traditional area of Taipei, just southwest of the city's governmental center. It is known as Wanhua (the 10,000 Glories). Of central interest is the Lung Shan (Dragon Mountain) Temple. Originally built in 1738, it has been rebuilt on several occasions, following fire, earthquake, and bombing. However it still retains a very traditional flavor. Because the temple was such an important social hub in centuries past, the area surrounding it became a bustling trade centre. Now it is best known as one of the 'licenced quarters' where prostitution is legally pursued. Snake Alley is also only one block away and is crowded every night with tourists, diners, and gawkers who come to see the vivisection of turtles and snakes served up fresh for culinary adventurers.

Jenai Road and Chunghsiao East Road

Over the past decade, this area has blossomed. Twenty years ago, Ling-li went to a new junior high school built in the area that was in the midst of a papaya and mango orchard. Now it is high-rise offices, apartments, hotels, memorials, and boutiques.

Traveling east from the Presidential Office Building on Chieh Wu Road, you will first hit the northwest corner of the Chiang Kai Shek Memorial. Step in and learn more about this important figure in modern Chinese history, then continue down Jenai Road. The tall and beautiful trees on this road and on Dunhua Road were left standing for a reason. It was the route taken from the Sungshan Airport to the Presidential Office Building when visiting American statesmen came to see how their foreign aid was being invested.

A long walk past hotels and boutiques will take you to the Sun Yat Sen Memorial Hall where this Chinese patriot is remembered. Jenai

Road comes to a dead end at Keelung Road and there, to your right, you will see the Hyatt Hotel and the striking pink marble World Trade Center. If there are any trade shows in progress, you can probably slip in as a 'visiting overseas buyer' and look at the vast array of goods being exported from Taiwan. If you go north on Keelung Road and return toward the city center on Chunghsiao Road, you will pass by the Ding Hao night market. Scores of boutiques, pubs, fast food restaurants, jewelry, and bookstores line this road.

The Chiang Kai Shek Memorial is one of the most famous landmarks in Taipei.

Tai Da Area

Tai Da is the popular abbreviation for Taiwan University, the most prestigious on the island. The cream of Taiwan's students rise to the top via the school testing systems and end up here studying law, medicine, science, etc. Adjacent to Tai Da is the Taiwan Normal University which prepares students to be teachers. With this concentration of young affluent academics, the area was destined to become a hub of culture in the city. Here you can find some modestly priced international restaurants and shopping bargains.

Along Ho Ping East Road fronting the University are some quaint teahouses serving Chinese tea and snacks. Along Roosevelt Road are bookstores. One block away from and parallel to Roosevelt Road is Ding Chow Street. Here you will find attractively priced international restaurants serving Thai, Burmese, Indonesian, and Vietnamese food.

In the towns around Taipei, you will also find many interesting sights on half-day and one-day excursions.

Gwan Du and Gwan Yin Mountain

The town of Gwan Du lies at the foot of Gwan Yin Mountain, about 30 minutes west of Taipei. The sun sets over the mountain, which is seen from Taipei as the reclining facial profile of the Goddess of Mercy. The Gwan Du Temple holds a lantern exhibition and competition during the Lantern Festival. There is a path to hike up the mountain and on its slopes and top you will find thousands of traditional graves. There is heavy traffic up and down the mountain on Tomb Sweeping Day.

Yangming Mountain Park, Seven Stars Mountain, and Matsau Hot Springs

North of the city is the pleasant drive up Yangmingshan. You will pass by the villas and houses of rich Taiwanese and expatriates working for foreign enterprises. You will also pass the University of Culture. From this area, you can take a detour to Seven Stars Mountain. There is a pleasant hiking path here, identified in several guide books for foreigners. Drive to the Yangming National Park and take a break. There are trails and a running stream with small waterfalls. It is a pleasant picnic area. When in full blossom in the spring, it gets quite crowded.

Continue driving up the mountain to Matsau. The winding road will take you along some breathtaking scenery, making you quickly forget that only 45 minutes ago you left behind a polluted and crowded city. Terraced tea and vegetable plantations appear by the side of the road as you drive to a pass in the mountains. Beyond this point you will start descending along the winding road and, on a clear day, will be able to see the golden beaches of Taiwan's north coast. Try to stop at the Matsau Hot Springs which is a rather nondescript place on your left. The greatest landmark will be the landslide that leaves the mountain ahead of you, gashed open and steaming from the geysers. At Matsau there is a very rustic but relaxing spot. For NT$40 you can get a cubicle with your own private bathtub and a rented towel. Soap is extra. The two crude taps control the water flow. Make it as hot as you can stand it and then soak in the mineral water. Silver and low carat gold jewelry will be discolored by the water, so remove them first. This is an excellent way to spend a cold winter's morning. Afterward, try the delicious sweet potato and ginger soup served at the canteen in the parking lot.

From Matsau, you can continue down the mountain to the Jinshan Beach recreation area, and from there to Keelung. You can return to Taipei along the highway, or you can retrace your tracks back to Taipei, perhaps taking the turnoff at Yangming Park that will lead you down the mountain to Peitou. Peitou was a famous R & R center for Japanese and, later, American military personnel, but its reputation as a den of iniquity is all but past. For a romantic evening with your own sweetheart, book a room at the quiet Whispering Pines Inn. It was built by the Japanese in Japanese-style with *tatamis*, *shojis*, and hot spring baths in each room.

National Palace Museum

A day excursion in itself, and definitely not to be missed, is the National Palace Museum, located a half hour north of the city. It houses some 600,000 artifacts, cataloged at the Forbidden City in Beijing, which were removed and guarded by Chiang Kai Shek's minions during a perilous 15-year journey through China and finally to Taiwan. There they were stored in underground bunkers until a modern museum could be erected. Now the National Palace Museum is the single most important repository of Chinese fine art in the world.

Porcelain, jade, scrolls, and bronze, all of the finest quality, are on display year round.

Jinshan and Fulung Beaches

About one and a half hour's drive from Taipei are two beaches, Jinshan and Fulung. If you like to bake in the sun and take in some moderate body surf, this is the place for you.

Central and East Taiwan

A weekend excursion can be made by car or bus along the northeast coast of Keelung, past the famous Yeliu Stone Formations. Here, where the land meets the sea, strange and attractive rock formations remain, carved over thousands of years by the wind and water. Incidentally, the naturally carved 'Empress's Head' bust was recently stolen by vandals, who later remorsefully returned it. It has now been cemented back into place.

Continue down past Suao to the turn-off for the interior of the island. Here you can drive through the beautiful Taroko Gorge. Steep cliffs rise up from a cold rushing mountain stream. You can stop at a temple situated nearby, enjoy the sights, and even get your picture taken with an aboriginal maiden.

After this, proceed to Tien Hsiang, a very quiet spot which is not too touristy. There are two places to stay: the Tien Hsiang Lodge and Father Paul's, a guest house. Here, deep in this green gorge, with the stars bright in a crystal-clear sky, you can spend a very quiet, relaxing evening. At dawn, walk or drive about three quarters of a mile further west along the main road. Look carefully for a path that goes down from the road to the rushing stream. You will cross a suspension bridge and continue down a rocky path to the water's edge. If you get here early enough, you will find yourself alone in the splendor of a natural outdoor hot spring that mixes with an ice-cold mountain stream.

If you have the time, continue west from Tien Hsiang to Lishan. This is a quaint orchard town. The scenery from the height of the narrow winding road is not for the queasy or the unsure driver. From here, drive north to the North Cross Island Highway, taking it west to pass Shihmen Reservoir and back to Taipei on the north-south Highway.

If you are an avid hiker, Taiwan has some of the best trails in North Asia. There are various clubs and associations that can put you on the right track. Taiwan is also a manufacturer of tents, boots, and all manner of hiking gear, so you can get what you need when you arrive.

Also on the east coast are opportunities to go white-water rafting. Check with tour guides for details.

The quiet beauty of the scenery in Tien Hsiang is a welcome contrast to the noise and bustle of Taipei.

201

Tainan

Tainan is the oldest city in Taiwan. It is also where Koxinga is buried. Here you can visit some of Taiwan's finest temples.

Kenting

If some cold winter morning you have a hankering for sun and sand, take a trip to Kenting. The journey is either a five-hour drive from Taipei, or can be made by plane and bus. This area, at the southern tip of the island, has an internationally managed resort, an underwater park, hiking trails, and beaches.

-Chapter Nine-

SHENGYI—THE MEANING OF LIFE

' "How is business?" I asked.

"Not good lah!" he chimed, his nicotine and betel-stained teeth forming a bloody grin. With the crash of the stock market, people were buying fewer of the car stereos sold by his small specialty shop located among a dozen other small specialty shops selling exactly the same thing. Business (*shengyi*) to Chinese is literally the meaning of life. Life was not too good, but his smile and nature were as easy as ever.'

—Conversation with a Taiwanese entrepreneur, from *Unwanted Vocabulary* by Chris Bates.

Taiwan has become an economic powerhouse, a geographically small, but flexible and adaptive player in the world manufacturing scene. It is, as mentioned in the first chapter, one of the most successful of the so-called 'Four Little Tigers of Asia', the other three being South Korea, Hong Kong, and Singapore. But Taiwan has not had the trouble with student protests and strikes that have plagued Korea. It is larger in population and land mass than Hong Kong and Singapore, giving it a larger pool of educated labor and room to spread out. In 1987, it recorded a trade surplus of U.S.$70 billion ($3,500 for every man, woman, and child on the island) and went on to become one of the richest nations in the world when measured by foreign exchange reserves. It also earned increased scrutiny from its trading partners, who were caught on the negative side of that trade imbalance.

So how could a diplomatically isolated, tiny island nation of over 20 million people generate enough momentum to be one of the top 10 trading nations in the world? First prepare the ground works with beneficial education, land reform, and investment policies. Add the fertilizer of foreign aid and investment, and technology transfer. Even with all this, your seed has to be strong and hardy. This is where the beliefs and cultural traditions of Taiwan have served it well. The shame-based culture, with its strongest source of influence being closest to the individual (i.e. his or her family), generates immediate feedback, a strong will to succeed, and a ability to sacrifice present comfort for future return to the family.

The Mandarin term *shengyi*, literally translated, means 'the meaning of life'. For most Taiwanese, then, the ultimate rewards of existence do not lie in heaven or enlightenment, but in the accumulation of wealth for the family. Indeed, we can view business as the fourth aspect of Taiwan's cultural tradition, equal in importance to Buddhism, Confucianism, and Taoism (see Chapter Five). If you understand that the people you are employing and associating with treat business this seriously, you will be a step further along the road toward successfully dealing with them.

You might interpret this to mean that the Taiwanese businessman is a 'family man' in the Western sense. You might even invite him to your house to show him how you get along with your children and provide for their needs (i.e. to show that you share a common goal with respect to your families). Know, though, that the Taiwanese businessman is very likely looking at your 12-year-old and wondering why he or she is listening to music, riding a bike, or playing video games instead of studying. The Taiwanese businessman does not acquire wealth to make his family necessarily more comfortable (though this is frequently a side effect). Rather, he does so to make them more productive, to provide his children with the environment and tools which will enable them, in turn, to create wealth that may be shared with him and his wife in their twilight years.

Let us review the postwar history of business in Taiwan, then look more closely at a typical Taiwanese business and how you should approach dealing with them.

THE ECONOMY OF TAIWAN

The island's basic infrastructure was mainly developed during the Japanese colonization. The population was sufficiently educated (albeit in Japanese) and, with Taiwan's retrocession at the end of World War II, the foundation was laid for one of Asia's postwar 'miracles'. After some initial fumbling, the Kuomintang got their act together and, in the 1950s, promoted agricultural extension services, crop research, and land reform which put ownership of regulated sizes of farm plots back in the hands of the farmers. At that time the bulk of Taiwan's work force was agricultural. The government established many *gung jya ji gwan* or 'public corporations', such as Taiwan Power, China Petroleum, China Steel, China Airlines, and RSEA (a construction company employing retired servicemen). These provided several boosts to the economy, namely, employment at a time when a massive influx of immigrants had arrived from Mainland China; stable and controlled commodity pricing; and a source of business for hundreds of small suppliers of tools, commodities, raw materials, and services to these large companies.

The economy slowly began to shift away from its agricultural base. Today, manufacturing and services share roughly equal levels of employment at 41 and 42 percent respectively, while agriculture has dropped to 17 percent. Textiles, clothing, electronics, processed foods, chemicals, steel, ships, and plastics became principal products.

In the 1960s and 70s, manufacturing was either backed by foreign investment or took the form of contract manufacturing in support of foreign manufacturers. Another growth industry at the time was pirate production, counterfeiting, and 'copy cat' manufacturing of lower quality goods for a limited local or regional market. China and Taiwan have no history of intellectual property protection. Indeed, if we look at China's arts and crafts, the tradition is to learn through rote and precise imitation of past masters, leading to mastery of tradition rather than mastery of expression. It has been argued that part of China's historical lack of success in capitalizing on the discoveries of its scientists and inventors was the absence of any way of protecting intellectual property. There was no incentive to invent beyond personal necessity.

In the 1980s, several important political and economic channels began to converge. Mainland China began to be seen as a credible (and cheaper) manufacturing alternative to the 'Four Tigers'. Western nations, and especially the United States, put pressure on Taiwan to correct its trade imbalance. The Cold War drew to a close and the United States began to actively withdraw its support for the one-party regimes it had backed during the long struggle with Communism.

The confluence of these macro-trends resulted in massive change for Taiwan. With the appreciation of the Taiwan dollar from NT$40 to NT$25 against U.S.$1, coupled with the ever more attractive choice of Mainland China for business, foreign manufacturers fled the island. Chris recalls in the mid-1980s that every time he changed clothes in the locker room of the American Club he would overhear businessmen discussing plans to pull their plants out of Taiwan.

Taiwanese industry had to rapidly shift gears. Manufacturers have done this in two ways. The less imaginative have pulled their plants out of Taiwan and followed the foreign manufacturers to Thailand, Malaysia, and China (which became an option with political liberalization). They are chasing cheap labor and the ability to continue producing mediocre to good quality products and assemblies on a contract manufacturing basis for other companies that own the designs and brands. More daring Taiwanese companies, however, are investing in creating a brand image with unique high quality product lines of their own and are trying to create their own branded sales channels. Companies like Acer, Tera, and UB are in this category. They feel that Taiwanese industry's only long-term chance for survival is to follow the example of major corporations in the industrialized world and develop, promote, and maintain proprietary corporate identities.

With this new local imperative, the cry has gone out to protect intellectual property. Now that Taiwanese corporations are producing intellectual property to protect, they want the backup of the legal system. Legislation was enacted in the late 1980s to step up investigation into counterfeiting activities and increase penalties for it. Although copy Rolex watches are still readily available, the pirate market is less of a free-for-all than it used to be.

What we have *not* seen, though, is a shift to the massive corporation, comparable to the Korean or Japanese development models. The government enterprises still operate and are now slowly being privatized. But only several large-scale Taiwanese corporations exist; Formosa Plastic and Evergreen Shipping come to mind. Even these companies, as big as they are today, were started by individual entrepreneurs. The rest of the economy is fueled by the entrepreneurial engine; there exist literally tens of thousands of small and medium-sized businesses. They manufacture, provide services, export, import, and trade. They have created a network of 'niche' players and copy cat artists.

The advantages of the small and medium-sized enterprise economy are:

- the smaller companies are more flexible and can change corporate direction 'on a dime'.
- they maintain low overheads and attempt to remain competitive at all costs because they are the life blood of the owners.
- tight control of overheads and margins allows them to remain competitive as a supplier of OEM sub-assemblies.

The disadvantages of the small and medium-sized enterprise economy are:

- they have limited research, marketing, and strategic planning resources.
- they maintain an over-dependency on the owner for decision-making.
- they do not develop the 'critical mass' necessary to be more than a component supplier.

Land of the Entrepreneur

It is a cultural imperative that drives the Chinese to be their own bosses. We believe it stems from the family focus of their vision of Confucianism. "Why should I dedicate my knowledge, skills, and resources to a company when my family can best benefit from them more directly?" they would argue. After sufficient knowledge has been acquired in a core business, they leave to start up on their own, frequently with seed capital from in-laws. Another possible reason for this tendency is that, in a society that is highly regulated by the family, a personal enterprise becomes an expression of and outlet for one's individuality. If one works for a company and one's family, one is only attached to external visions of the self. Setting up one's own company allows the creation of a unique vision of oneself, over which one can exert maximum control.

Of course, not all Taiwanese break off to set up on their own, otherwise no publicly-listed corporation could survive! But it is a significant cultural trait. More successful small and medium-sized enterprises try to prevent the exodus of their top managers with 'golden handcuffs' and stock ownership incentives.

All in the Family

The predominance of small and medium-sized firms leads to another phenomenon: nepotism. The word is usually used negatively in the West, but in Taiwan it is considered natural and necessary. "Who else can I trust?" is the question in the businessman's mind. "Certainly not someone from outside my family. And why should I let another family benefit anyway?" You will frequently find companies wherein the wife is the accounts or finance manager and the younger brother is the export sales manager, his MBA studies abroad having been financed by the older brother.

This scenario also facilitates more shady activities, such as maintaining two sets of books to reduce taxation. If you are investigating the credit-worthiness of a company that has reason to cooperate with you (such as a distributor or supplier), ask for a set of their accounts. Then have a credit bureau supply you with another set. Compare them and feel free to ask unpointed questions about discrepancies.

If you are running a company, it is best to discourage or even ban the hiring of relatives. This is a preventive measure which reduces the possibility that they will work together to put their family interests before company interests. If you don't take this precaution, you may see the effects of nepotism manifesting themselves in areas like hiring, contract approval, accounts anomalies, missing inventory, and disappearing customers. It also precludes several related people from acquiring enough information about your business to quit together and readily set up as a successful competitor. For one employee to successfully do this alone, he or she would probably have risen through the ranks to acquire the perspective of several middle managers. By the time your higher employees do this, you should have been able to identify him or her as a 'comer' and cement a long-term relationship with stock or bonus incentives.

Do not feel that this is harsh or discriminatory toward the Taiwanese family value system. Such an opinion is typical of the 'straight, gullible, naive' approach with which the Chinese stereotype Westerners (mentioned in Chapter Six). One company I worked with had several members from three families in the management, but there was a standing rule against staff marrying or even dating. If you wanted to date, one of you had to go. Another company established by four unrelated partners had a standing rule covering all personnel that no relatives could be employed. Tell your staff that you will not employ your nephew from Arkansas or Minsk and they will not employ their wife, brother, sister, cousin, etc.

AN APPOINTMENT WITH A TYPICAL TAIWANESE COMPANY

As with all things in life, there is never an absolute 'typical'. However, there are experiences and perceptions which, when repeated over and over again, give one a feel for the typical in aggregate. We mentioned above that Taiwan's economy has bred a vast sea of small and medium-sized enterprises which support each other, support foreign buyers, and support the larger Taiwanese companies.

These enterprises are normally started by one man (occasionally a woman or husband-and-wife team) who has garnered some practical experience from a former employer and sets out on his own, in some way, to repeat the success he has observed. They start out modestly with little capital and long hard hours of work. But they succeed and slowly build the business up. Among these enterprises, it is rare to see a corporate identity or office ambiance. Only the visionary companies, or those looking at selling out, have one. For sure, you may visit much larger and modern corporations with conditions that are most opulent and 'Western', but if you visit any of their suppliers, you will then see the typical company, which we will now visit.

The Pick-up

You have made an appointment to see Mr. Fliver Chen, President of Wholesome Goodies Ltd. Fearing that you cannot find his office in its out-of-the-way place, he personally comes to your hotel to pick you up. Despite the fact he has had to drive in 70 minutes of downtown traffic, he arrives only 10 minutes late. The hotel receptionist points you out to him, he comes over with a big smile on his face, and then firmly shakes your hand, introducing himself in English and extending a name card to you. You take his card in both hands, examine it carefully, and thank him for giving it to you, extending one of your own to him in return.

He is dressed in a European-style, short-sleeved shirt with an open collar, slacks, and scuffed leather shoes (it's impossible to keep shoes clean between the dust, debris, and damp in Taiwan). He is carrying a *dageda* (cellular phone) and a large bunch of keys. He beckons you to come out to his waiting car. He has given you face by coming personally to fetch you and you thank him for this undeserved attention.

You sit in the front seat of his Volvo 760 and the air-conditioning quickly cuts through your shirt, making you chill. He has an imported radio cassette player on which he is playing Western classical music. As the car pulls out into the traffic, he asks you if this is your first trip to Taiwan, what you think of the traffic, the food, etc.

During the hour-long start-and-stop drive to his office, the conversation is mostly social. He wants to get to know you. So, you should use the opportunity to get to know him. Feel free to ask of him any question he has asked of you: sports, travel, family, how he came to know you or your company, your schedule.

Finally, he pulls through a red metal gate in a high gray concrete wall. A painted brass company plaque is affixed to the wall, proclaiming the home of 'Wholesome Goodies'. There is not much maneuvering room in the parking area but he takes a space reserved for his car near the front door.

The Building

You enter the building through a sliding glass door. Inside, on the ground level, are eight desks, carefully arranged to fit in an area of about 800 square feet. The floor is made of a composite of concrete and stone chips, and is polished and gray. Several fans with blue blades, not recently cleaned, are mounted to the walls. They swing back and forth, distributing a breeze through the office. Against the walls around the room are filing cabinets, catalog shelves, a fax machine, a copy machine, an aquarium with one large sleek fish, and a bottled water dispenser. Seated at four of the desks are office girls. They have computers or typewriters on their desks and look busy. Two of the other desks are empty and two are occupied by younger men wearing ties who are reading the morning newspapers.

Mr. Chen leads you upstairs to his office. The second level was carpeted long ago and trails now show where the heaviest traffic flows. You are left in a small meeting room and the window air-conditioner is turned on. Mr. Chen excuses himself. You are sitting on a low sofa with a coffee table in front of you. You are probably uncomfortable, finding your knees up against your chest.

As the room cools down you look around. There is a colorful calendar from a Japanese supplier on one wall. On the wall facing you, hanging high near the ceiling, is a black carved wooden plaque with gold leaf Chinese characters on it. It is an expression of good fortune, given to the company on its founding day many years ago. On the coffee table is a marble ashtray, cigarette lighter, and humidor set, placed atop a lace doily. Under the coffee table are industrial magazines and catalogs.

A secretary appears and asks whether you would like tea or coffee. You tell her your choice and she disappears again. Mr. Chen shortly returns and apologizes for having had to make several calls.

The secretary presents your drink and retreats, leaving you and the boss to talk.

The Meeting

Depending on the nature of *your* business and the nature of *his* business, the meeting can take many different directions at this point. Very probably he will introduce you to his lieutenants and you will have a detailed discussion about the prospects of your respective companies doing business. If he has a factory and it is located in the same place as the office, he will probably be happy to let you tour it. There will inevitably be difficulties in language, but a smile and some patience will give all parties the time to find a way of expressing the point in a different way.

During the meeting, the accountant brings in a small stack of papers for Mr. Chen to 'chop' (see Chapter Four). He excuses himself, looks over each one carefully, but not excessively, then chops each one in the appropriate place with his seal and red ink. It is very possible that Mrs. Chen also works in the company, very possibly as the finance or accounts manager.

Mr. Chen is clearly 'the boss'. The company revolves around him. He listens to his lieutenants' input and your thoughts, but the decision is his to make. Indeed, to insist in a challenging way that he must accept your point of view would be disastrous. Better to wait for a quiet moment alone after a few drinks to express your respect for the strength of his convictions, but that you feel it is in his company's best interest to follow your suggestions.

Lunch and Siesta

The discussions have gone well and it is way past noon. Mr. Chen says they have planned a lunch for you. He invites his right-hand man to attend and you all head downstairs. The lights are out and you notice a macabre sight: formless bodies slouched at each desk. One of the secretaries pulls her coat from her head and you now know this is the

213

syousyi or *wushwei* (siesta period after lunch). The office staff have put their coats over their heads and are resting on the desks. At 1:30 p.m. the lights will come back on and the office will reanimate.

You have told Mr. Chen that you love Chinese food, so lunch is at a pleasant air-conditioned eatery, not far away. Beer is served, but it is evident that the Taiwanese want to save the heavy drinking for the evening. Several cold appetizers are quickly brought to the table including peanuts, *doufu* threads with shredded carrots and celery, and marinated clams fragrant with soy sauce, garlic, and chilli. Sanitary wooden chopsticks (*weisheng kwaidz*) are used, which everyone ceremoniously snaps apart like wishbones. Mr. Chen is a modern fellow and asks the waitress to bring chopsticks and spoons solely for serving purposes.

Several hot courses of seafood, meat, and vegetables are brought to the table, accompanied by white steamed rice. A soup is also delivered. A dessert of fresh fruit follows.

Mr. Chen's lieutenant is asked to drive you back to your hotel. Before parting, Mr. Chen asks whether you are free that evening. You respond that you are and would like to invite him out. He insists that you be his guest and a time is set to pick you up. Smiles and thanks follow, and you return to your hotel.

NETWORKING TAIWANESE-STYLE

How would you have made contact with Mr. Chen? You arrived in Taiwan and knew no one. How do you set up?

It is very important that you get to know people as soon as possible. The recent buzzword from the U.S. is 'networking' and Taiwan is certainly a highly networked society. The family is the first channel of networking. So, if you don't have family in Taiwan, then you will have to develop contacts.

The importance of generating and cultivating contacts cannot be over-stressed. In Taiwan, this is called *gwan syi* and means 'relations'. Of course, you must maintain 'good relations' with everyone, from your hired help onward. But this is not the real Taiwanese meaning. Good *gwan syi* is developed with people normally at your level or above in the social and business hierarchy; in other words, with those people who can instruct or obstruct, decide or desist, nod or shake. Good *gwan syi* opens doors, smoothes out troubles, leads to further *gwan syi*, ad infinitum. It is a web that grows. Just as a spider tends to its web and keeps it in good repair and working order, so too your network must not be neglected. Think of it as networking, with the cultural imperatives layered on, and you will find it an easier task.

The type of contacts you will need to develop will vary depending on your purpose in coming to Taiwan. You can begin to generate contacts by visiting organizations like your country's Chamber of Commerce or Business Association. Some businessmen will be able to make beneficial contacts through the China External Trade Development Council (CETRA) and other ROC trade organizations. There are a variety of specific industrial associations, the Taiwan Spectacles Manufacturers Association, for example. However, this type of association will probably not have fluent English speakers, so you must be prepared to organize help in that area. In addition, your friends, associates of sister companies, or even your corporate attorney or auditor may also provide a useful lead that provides another lead that moves you in the right direction.

As you construct your web of contacts, maintain it. Sending thanyou notes to people who introduced you to people, follow-up calls, perhaps an invitation to dinner or golf would justify their confidence in helping you express your sincere gratitude; and earn *ren ching wei* points. If any of your contacts calls you back, do not dismiss them or not return the call. Yes, they probably want something, but it may be help you can provide, or a contact you can offer, which will one day be returned. The web strengthens.

As illustrated in our visit to a Taiwanese company, certain behavior will make the Taiwanese more comfortable with you (see Chapter Six). Dress as formally as dictated by your business. If you are overdressed, you can slowly loosen up, so it is better to err on the side of conservatism.

Name Cards

The exchange of name cards is a simple ritual that must not be neglected. Like the Japanese, the Taiwanese value name cards. They are the physical reminder of one's *gwan syi*. The exchange of cards is not a new thing in China; it was certainly used in the last century, if not earlier. The use of a written description of one's position or status, usually prepared by a government official to bestow status or power, is millennia old. A person might give you their card to take when visiting another person. It conveys their *gwan syi*.

Treat the name card of the person you meet with the deference you give the man (or woman) himself. Look at it closely, study it, understand their title and name, and comment on their company's corporate identity if it is nice or new. Do not make the same mistake as the culturally clumsy American vice president of Chris' acquaintance who offended the Chinese customers he met by collecting a stack of name cards like scrap paper and then dealing out his name cards across the table back to the guests like a brusque Las Vegas croupier. Also, do not run out of cards. In a busy week of networking or sales it is easy to go through 100 cards. Also consider getting a Chinese name (see Chapter Four).

Be agreeable and inquisitive. Be concerned about the person you are meeting and their company. Be frank, open, relaxed, unhurried, and well-rounded. At the same time, remember that until a relation is well-established, you will not want to be too liberal in 'tipping your hand'. On the other hand, do not be overly secretive either. Sounds like a fine line to draw, doesn't it? Try to avoid giving answers like, "I am sorry, I cannot tell you. It's confidential information." You are telling the person in a direct and perhaps face-losing way that you do not trust them or their company. The Taiwanese would say the same thing much more indirectly, for instance, "The information is not ready yet. Can I get you a copy when it's finished?" The person spoken to may or may not expect to get the information later.

What Do They Expect From You?

So, what is a Taiwanese businessperson looking for in their relationship with a foreigner? Whether you are buying or selling, we feel that what they seek can be summarized in order of importance as follows:

1. *Maximization of profits.* The Taiwanese businessperson will naturally try to maximize their profits in their relations with you. If you are selling, they will squeeze for price, or terms, or consignment, or all three. Explain how they can profit from your current sales package and what you will do to see that the program is a success. Do as much background checking as possible to verify or discount their claims that a price break is needed for them to be able to profit. Then make your proposal to your management, or make the decision yourself, whichever is appropriate. If you are buying from them, you will probably be promised the moon and receive the late delivery of something less!

2. *Dealings on the right level.* The Taiwanese are very conscious of hierarchy. Based on their own cultural perspective, a person ranked too low will be seen as ineffectual or a stepping stone, rather than a conduit to working with your office. Not knowing you, they will give you the benefit of the doubt at first. If you are not empowered to make decisions and do not establish good *gwan syi* with your business ties, they will go around you. Of course, they can tolerate the occasional, "I'll have to check with headquarters," but not consistently.

3. *Long-term relations.* The Taiwanese business partner would much rather have the opportunity of establishing a long-term relationship with you, rather than a one-off. It saves them having to understand yet another raft-load of foreigners if they change supplier or customer; it allows them to exercise *gwan syi* to the fullest; and it smoothes out their long-term cash flow projections.

4. *Friendship.* Though it may take several years, your business

217

contact will hope to eventually make friends with you. The Taiwanese are friendly, relaxed folk. The friendship will mature after many shared experiences and hardships.

Bribery, Corruption, Grease, and Gifts

Yes, *hung bau* do still exist. So does bribery. And, no, it is not absolutely necessary. In fact, the book *Doing Business in Taiwan* (see Bibliography) indicates that, in resolving questions of legality, a resort to bribery and *gwan syi* may be disastrous. If your case is strong, the law will prevail. Other sources also indicate that Western companies which operate within the law and which successfully resist opportunities to bribe and corrupt, are able to get the business on the merit of their offer. We agree and disagree.

Let us play a little 'line-drawing' game here. Where does a gift become a bribe? Although not a legal opinion, a bribe is a substantial inducement given (usually after the event) to guarantee the outcome of an event. A gift, on the other hand, is a token of esteem used to cement friendly relations and express sincerity. It is usually given before the outcome of the event is known and with no guarantee as to the outcome being expressed.

Taiwanese are emotional people. They have a finely-tuned social awareness. If they do not like you or your company for some emotional reason, they see no reason to favor your offers. They should feel that you and your company are the right ones to deal with. Giving a gift the wrong way, to the wrong person, or indeed giving the wrong gift, can be more disastrous than not giving one at all. Do not treat gifts as bribes or inducements. Get to know the person with whom you want to establish good relations and understand their needs and fears (they have some vision for their department, factory, company). Then treat the gift as something given freely, without coercion, between friends.

If you do not get the business, do not collar the fellow and ask pointedly why you did not get the contract. Instead, invite him out again, ask in what ways your company's offer can be improved in the future, and whether there are any other jobs you can approach him for. Strengthen the network. Who knows? He may even tell you that all is not lost and he is willing to re-open the bidding.

MANAGING TAIWANESE STAFF

You have read Chapter Five and have begun to understand what the Taiwanese think of you. As you are a foreign manager, they will have certain conceptions about how you will work with them and operate the company. Many Taiwanese express relief when working for Western companies because structured chances for advancement exist, doors are open, and the pay is marginally better. You do not have to stomp in like your conception of a paternalistic, autocratic, Taiwanese, family-owned business manager to make them feel comfortable.

However, sympathy and understanding of the dynamics of Taiwanese interpersonal relations are important. First, understand what you represent to them. You are the 'boss', the *lau ban*, or if you are a woman, the 'bossette', *lau ban niang*. You are expected to retain an air of control and respectability. Do not show panic or discomfort. Show displeasure only when you can express it privately and in such a way as not to make the person lose face. The Western penchant for the snide, the satirical comment, or backhanded compliment is not appreciated. When they understand, it is resented, otherwise it is generally not understood. Remember the Western management maxim 'Criticize in Private, Praise in Public', but choose your words simply and without ambiguity.

Getting Your Staff Involved

A frequent difficulty expressed by Western managers in Taiwan is getting their staff to 'open up'. Remember again that Taiwan has a shamed-based culture. People are motivated by trying to avoid being shamed. If you call a staff meeting and find yourself giving a monologue, you need to draw out or begin to tap your managers'

219

reserves of creativity and individuality. They do not want to criticize others in public for fear of reprisals and do not want to stick their necks out with new risky ideas either.

Opening them up can be done in several ways. If the company is large and the problem great, you can hire a management consultant to help facilitate the blossoming of your staff. On the other hand, if your office is small, you can initiate change yourself. Start with private meetings. Ask about the person's past (college, team sports, career) and aspirations. What do they like about the company? Explain that you are not Taiwanese, but you feel you understand that they are concerned about not taking a risk by extending opinions. You understand. At the same time, you come from a different culture, one which may reward risk-takers, even when they fail, because having learned a valuable lesson they will do much better the next time. Perhaps you could offer an example from your own history. You also come from a culture where individuals succeed in teams. Explain that the rules of success in your company are based on participation, cooperation, and risk-taking. Ask the person to think about this.

At the next staff meeting, remind everyone of your conversation and then perhaps bring up something good that has come up during the week that was done by the managers working as a team. Thank them for that. Then bring up something done by an individual that showed merit and point out why it is of mention. Then bring up a topic that you feel needs to be urgently addressed, perhaps one that is on your desk, not theirs. Ask for their input on the proper solution. Do not criticize any of the proposals, but rather express how and in what way it has shed light on some aspect of the problem that was not evident before. In other words, even wrong answers have merit. Because it is a problem on your desk, a decision need not be made on the spot—no judgement required.

It will take time and many meetings to open up your staff. It is most important, though, to create an environment where they feel safe to do so. Remember, however, that you are ultimately in command and are expected to provide the example of leadership.

Gossip

Gossipmongering is a frequent problem in Taiwanese companies and creates and perpetuates ill-will between staff. The bad thing is that your Mandarin may not pass muster yet and the gossip could be about you! It is very important that you have a local person on your staff whom you feel you can trust more fully, someone who can be your eyes and ears in the organization. This might be your personnel or accounts manager. If you have a really large organization, choose more than one person for this job. Take your staff out to socialize and loosen up. Dinner, drinking, or golf with a customer are good choices. Share some good times and some adventure with them. This in itself may slow the rumor mill about you and get you valuable insights into the human resource at your command.

Intermediaries

One time-honored Taiwanese tradition you can effectively employ is the use of an intermediary. If an employee is having a problem or under-performing, you might use the 'eyes and ears' mentioned above to communicate with the party in question. This saves that person losing face in front of you when explaining their problem.

Ren Ching Wei

Ren ching wei is also very important. Feelings and emotions are the power of human and corporate relationships in Taiwan, not duty or obligation. All the more so in times of high employment, when staff can walk across the street for a slightly higher paying job because they do not like the feeling they have around you. Do you inspire confidence, loyalty, and direction? Can they feel that you understand them and their motivations, both personal and cultural? When they come to work with a white ragged armband pinned around their sleeve, do you ask them to remove it before going out to see an important customer, or do you inquire as to who died and express condolences?

Corruption

Be on your guard against dishonesty, corruption, or thieving within the ranks. This is not to say that Taiwanese are overly dishonest, corrupt, or thieving. It takes place in every culture, in every country. But you are a stranger here. You do not understand the language. You do not know what the hell is going on around you, even under your very nose. Install proper corporate procedures for accounting, personnel, and management. Use as much as you can from your headquarters manual. Then, when you are comfortable that you are in control of your business, feel free to 'tweak' the system to make it fit your Taiwanese staff just right. Loosen up just enough.

BUSINESS SAFEGUARDS

Let's say you want to procure half a million pieces of a unique patented alarm clock radio designed by your company. You may wish to install certain safeguards. There are lots of middlemen in Taiwan, so ask if the person you are talking to is a middleman. If he is not, ask where his factory is and if you can tour it. Try to get straight to the manufacturer. The person you are dealing with may only make the plastic moulded shell and have the printed circuit board made outside. In that case, you may want to also insist on a meeting with the PCB manufacturer at his factory.

When you have set on a supplier, you will need to try to protect yourself from a design copyright or patent perspective. Pirating is not the free-for-all it once was, but take the measures the law affords you. The patent registration procedure is covered fully in English in the book *Doing Business in Taiwan* (see Bibiliography).

You will have a contract that covers technical specifications, returns, terms, delivery dates, etc. It is legal and valid and is necessary for due diligence, but, ultimately, choosing the right supplier is a matter of choosing the right supplier. Roping the wrong guy into the right contract will bring you nothing but misery.

Finally, unless you have facilities or headquarters personnel who can perform the inspection of the goods at several stages of manufacture, then you should hire one of the many specialized service firms (many run by Westerners) which can provide inspection services.

BUSINESS SOCIALIZING AND ENTERTAINMENT

Now for the fun part: wining, dining, hitting little white balls around large green fields, and loosening your tie with some of Asia's most practiced 'good ol' boys'. The Taiwanese like to entertain and be entertained. They like loud restaurants, saucy stories, and they admire a person who can hold their liquor. Unfortunately, none of this is as economical as it once was. In fact, it is downright expensive. Make sure that your company has budgeted sufficiently for entertainment. Depending on the company size, even several percent of gross revenue might not be too much.

Daytime entertainment is restricted to lunches and golf. If you are a golfer, take advantage of the fact and do some business on the greens. It would not be appropriate to actually discuss business during the game, but the saunas, coffee shops, or dinner that come afterward offer many opportunities. The important thing is that you have a shared experience to help cement your business relationship.

Evening offers even more entertainment opportunities. A typical full-blown evening might comprise a grand dinner with beer or Chinese wine, retiring to a karaoke lounge to drink more, sing some songs, and converse with a hostess or two, followed by a midnight snack. This might be at Di Hwa Jye where Snake Alley and Lungshan Temple are located, or it might be at a coffee shop or night market.

Taiwanese enjoy drinking games. These are all loud, boisterous, and insanely fun competitions...if you are a drinker! The simplest game is the famous 'paper, scissors, rock' game. Slightly more complicated is another game of hand signs, whereby the participants quickly and simultaneously show a random number of fingers on one hand, while both shouting out the number they guess the sum of the two hands will form. If they are both wrong, the sequence is repeated, but if one of them is correct the loser has to take a shot. Aficionados will play this game with lightning speed, that is, until the effect of the alcohol takes it toll! Other experts will also say code words (like the city name 'Ilan' rather than the number *yi*, 'one'), making the game even funnier. The most complicated version we have seen involves the use of two hands for each participant. Keep in mind that repetitions are frequent and, to the uninitiated, it all sounds like a harried auctioneer calling out numbers. Through the haze of alcohol, the waving hands and voices blur. You will invariably lose more and more as the evening progresses.

The 'Face' of Entertaining

Whether you are being entertained or are entertaining, do not forget the importance of face. If being entertained, make sure the host knows you are enjoying yourself. To act otherwise would not only mark you as an ingrate, but make him lose face as well. Allow yourself to trust your host completely, even enough to let the two of you drink yourselves to the point of slap-happy oblivion (although not vomiting hysteria) if you are both so inclined. If you allow him to feel as though he has introduced you to an exotic experience, it will certainly draw the two of you closer.

When entertaining, remember face. If you invite the guests to a Chinese dinner, either let them order what they like, or have one of your local employees do so. If inviting them out for Western food, keep in mind that they may not be familiar with the kinds of food offered on the menu, or with special dining utensils, such as escargot clips, or a place setting of three knives and forks. This could be embarrassing to them. In such a situation, initiate an explanation of the cuisine to them. Don't patronize them with a set of instructions for boors, but give instead an emotional rendering of why you like this food, why you want to introduce them to it, and what it's all about. Don't opt for heavy-going Western foods which are usually considered an 'acquired taste' (Blue Stilton cheese, for instance). And be prepared to order for yourself something you think they would like, as they may feel compelled to order the same as you. If you recommend certain dishes to them, you should order one of them yourself.

Monkey Business

Taiwan is not the 'male paradise' it was once considered to be by businessmen seeking bedroom amenities while on the road. However, the Japanese and Taiwanese men still look for female company here, so it is readily available. As the 'Taipei A-Z Guide' in the back of *Taipei Living* comments, "There are many different types of barber shop in Taipei. Those listed below cut hair *only*." Indeed, you will find that along the length of Jilin Road and its side streets are hundreds of barber shops, in total employing as many as 20,000 women. How could there possibly be such a market for hair care? Simply put, the women do cut hair and give manicures, but the private rooms and reclining chairs are put to more extensive use. For a big tip you will probably end up with more than a haircut!

Hostesses are found in many karaoke and hostess lounges. Be aware that you are charged per girl for the amount of time they chat with you. Of course, you pay for their drinks as well, so bills run up quickly. Unless you or your guest really enjoy this sort of company, it may be better to opt for entertainment in one of the several 'pubs' which are advertised. These tend to be more like a Western bar or pub, and comprise lots of laughing, darts, and beer.

For the Businesswoman

It is quite possible for women to succeed in business in Taiwan. The current head of Yueloong Motors (Taiwan's automobile company) is, in fact, a woman. For a foreign woman, all the lessons already discussed in this book still apply, but there are also a few more tips.

As we have said, entertainment is an important part of making contacts, developing *gwan syi*, showing *ren ching wei*, and getting business. Obviously, Taiwanese (and probably expatriate) men would be uneasy at your presence with them at a 'barber shop'. But you can successfully entertain. Golfing would be a great alternative, especially if you are a good player and can give them a run for their money. Dinners are innocuous and if you are a good drinker they will be impressed. However, the extent to which you want to become 'one of the guys' will probably not be misconstrued in a romantic way if you draw clear boundaries. Karaoke bars (with or without hostesses) will relieve you from the possibility of having to dance with one of your guests if that makes you uncomfortable or is inappropriate. If it is a hostess bar, do not be embarrassed or think that they equate you, as a working woman, with 'working women' in the traditional sense. Indeed, they treat hostesses themselves as entertainers, not prostitutes. The banter with these women is sometimes saucy, with *double entendres* and innuendo, but it is rarely raunchy. It is not very common to see men leaving the bar with a hostess either.

A final word: if you are a general manager, take note that your calm resolve, ability to think through problems, and provision of acculturated leadership will be under constant scrutiny by your staff, even when entertaining.

Have a good time in Taiwan. Live long and prosper!

–*Chapter Ten*–

STAYING HEALTHY AND
HANDLING EMERGENCIES

"The doctor was a tired, overworked man who had just peered down at least one hundred throats and two hundred ears, had sprayed and swabbed all of them with the same elixir, and sent the patients on their way with a prescription and an admonition. Behind him were the tools of his trade: a reclining seat, various stainless steel bowls, stainless steel tools bathing in sterilizing fluid, and stainless steel sprayers and suction devices. We were the last patients of the morning shift."
—Taipei clinic scene, from *Unwanted Vocabulary* by Chris Bates.

227

As so many platitudes have proclaimed, prevention is easier than cure. However, when you find yourself in a foreign land, not only are many dangers alien to you, but the handling of possible emergencies is also different. Our advice, then, is to read this chapter before you have any necessity for the information contained.

HEALTH

It is easy to let your health deteriorate when you move to a foreign country. You arrive and have jet lag, new routines, new demands, and maybe an initial bout of intestinal flu. You go to bed every night feeling spent. You wake up facing a frustrating day ahead. On top of this you are experiencing culture shock.

Be kind and gentle on yourself. Take time to recover from illness. Force yourself to change your pace so you can finish the race, rather than letting the race finish you. Try to maintain your usual exercise routine. If you jogged, or played tennis or golf at home, find out about clubs and facilities open to you in Taiwan. Get into the network of new friends and associates with whom you can share your interests.

The climate is probably different in Taiwan than in your home country. It is hot and very humid in the summer, not affording many natural options for cooling down. People come to depend on air-conditioning, but this can lead to 'summer colds'. To prevent these, follow the local custom and learn to wear undergarments year round (see Chapter Three, *The Ubiquitous T-shirt*). Winter is troublesome because most homes and many offices are not heated. Again, you must learn to mix and match several layers of attire to stay in good health.

Water

Water is a basic element required in copious amounts by everyone living in Taiwan. The country is very hot in the summer and it is important that you do not become dehydrated. But, in answer to the never-ending question, "Is the water safe to drink?", the Taiwanese themselves never drink tap water that has not first been boiled or filtered. Chris drank unboiled tap water in Peitou for years without ill effect. However, we do not encourage you to try it.

Besides bacteria and viruses, a more subtle but no less dangerous component of the water might be chemicals (such as complex pesticides) and heavy metals. These cannot be removed by boiling and are not passed through the system. They accumulate in the body and, therefore, even trace amounts over time can become deleterious to your system. Filtering and boiling is recommended for cooking and drinking water. Many locals and expatriates have bottled water delivered to their premises. Check on the supplier of the bottled water and do shop around. Some suppliers have been hit on by the health authorities and consumer associations for supplying water which is sub-standard to the tap variety!

Food

As with all things, there is a *yin* and a *yang* to food. During your immersion in Taiwan, food can be a source of life-giving vitality, or a draining, energy-sapping scourge.

The locally available foods are, by and large, very healthy. Delicious fresh fruit and vegetables are various and plentiful. They will provide you with nourishment, roughage, and vitamins. It is important, however, that they are cleaned properly before consumption. In Taiwan, it is still customary to protect small vegetable plots with chemicals and fertilize them with unprocessed natural fertilizer (human and pig night soil). Until only recently, DDT was being used in Taiwan, and other very harsh and environmentally unsound chemicals can still be found. Vegetables should be soaked, washed, and cooked thoroughly. We have not had stomach problems with salad ingredients, providing they are properly cleaned. Fruit should also be soaked and washed, but can be eaten raw.

The Taiwanese commonly rinse off a fresh piece of meat or seafood bought from the vegetable market (see Chapter Three) prior to freezing it. We second this custom. You can buy freezer bags at the market. All meat and seafood should be thoroughly cooked, unless, of course, you are having *sushi* and *sashimi* (Japanese raw fish recipes). With regard to the latter, however, we suggest you follow the advice of an old Japan-hand, and only eat these dishes in the winter. In the summer, the ambient temperatures during the transportation of the catch from the fishing boat to the distributor to the wholesaler to the restaurant are guaranteed to make freshness questionable. *Sashimi* must be just-dead fresh.

Also be aware that buffets, cafeterias, and roadside stalls, though they may have a different ambience and different pricetags, can all serve up food that is tainted. This is not to say you should avoid them like the plague, but rather use caution in your selection of foods from them. It is always best to eat food that you are reasonably assured has been recently cooked or can be cooked to order.

At buffets, avoid eggs, mayonnaise, and foods that have a glazed-over or stale look. A friend came down with his worst case of intestinal

Taiwan, famous for its pork, reputedly has some of the 'cleanest' pigs in the world.

flu shortly after having a breakfast buffet at a major five-star hotel. He ordered an omelette to be prepared to his taste. Raw whipped eggs were poured into a pan from a pitcher but, while cooked to his liking, the inside of the omelette was not well done and the eggs were obviously not fresh.

Having said this, Chris also attended a buffet at a hotel restaurant and experienced something entirely different. At the end of the buffet was a carving table with a huge baked ham on the bone. When Chris got to the chef he was surprised to find him asking how he would like the meat (medium-rare or well done) as if it was a piece of beef. Chris declined to make a choice, but asked his business counterpart to advise him. He was told that Taiwan has some of the world's healthiest pigs which do not have the diseases (i.e. trichinosis) that must be cooked out of American pigs. Let the diner take their own risks where this is concerned! However, if you do want to choose how your meat is cooked, note that the Taiwanese do not actually use the terms 'medium' or 'well done'. They use a point system and literally ask, "How many points done?" Ten points is well done, seven to eight points is medium, and four to five points is rare. To tell the waiter your request you will need to learn the numbers from the primer in Chapter Four.

Another thing to be aware of in Taiwanese cuisine is a food additive called monosodium glutamate (MSG). This tenderizer and seasoning is sometimes used as a flavor enhancer in Western food, but it was invented in the Orient and is known locally as *weijing* (flavor essence). It is used by restaurants in copious amounts, being sprinkled over the food like salt during marination or cooking. Some people develop a reaction to MSG, which often takes the form of a runny nose and eyes soon after eating food which contains the flavoring. If you are sensitive to it, you may ask chefs not to use it in your dishes. Say, "*Ching bu yau jya weijing.*"

It is a good idea to bring your favorite stomach remedy with you from home. Products like Pepto-Bismol, Kaopectate, and Alka-

Seltzer are not as readily available in Taiwan as they are in the West. However, an excellent local remedy for vomiting and diarrhea is *baujiwan*. This traditional herbal preparation comes in convenient plastic vials. Take the whole vial of tiny brown pills in one gulp with a glass of warm water. However, if your vomiting or diarrhea occurs more than three times, you should try to see a doctor. Be sure to replace lost body fluids rapidly.

Pollution

The city of Taipei is geographically set in a 'bowl' surrounded by mountains. In fact, this positioning once prompted a friend of mine to quip during my visit to Taipei, "So, when are you 'flushing out' of this place?" The point is that, being set in a basin surrounded by mountains, Taipei holds in the fumes from traffic, industry, and cooking. These build up until they choke even the insensitive and weaken the strong.

It is therefore conceivable that your usual morning jog would become excruciating in downtown Taipei, as well as hazardous from the traffic point of view. Try getting up very early (like the Taiwanese do) to exercise in the parks before the pollution count gets too high.

If you jog or ride a bike or motorcycle, you may want to adopt the local custom of wearing a gauze face mask and glasses. Although the masks are too coarse to stop gaseous pollutants, they do prevent granular media from getting lodged in your nose, lungs, and eyes.

If you are a contact lens wearer, wash your lenses religiously and carry a bottle of eye drops with you at all times—you will definitely need them!

Smoke Stack City

The Taiwanese like to smoke cigarettes. The habit is common among young men. Most women do not smoke because it was formerly associated with vice among women. One of the friendliest and most common ice-breakers a Taiwanese will use with a foreigner who does not speak Chinese is to hoist out a pack of butts and proffer one. To scowl and refuse, as some non-smokers in the West might, would be seen as rude and devoid of cultural flexibility. The most polite refusal is to hold the outstretched fingers of your hand to your lips, as if you are making a one-handed prayer. While doing this, bow your head and say, "*Syesye, wo bu syi yan*" (Thank you, I do not smoke).

Some local companies have gone smoke-free in their offices and offered incentives for employees to 'kick the habit'. If you are the manager of your operation and appreciate a smoke-free environment, you can implement this policy without being seen as an eccentric Westerner.

Diseases

Conjunctivitis is a severe eye inflammation caused by reaction to airborne pollutants. Also known as 'pink eye', it is highly contagious. Considering what we have just said about pollution in Taipei, it would not be surprising if you contracted this complaint. We have found that over-the-counter preparations, like Bausch and Lomb Allergy Drops, can put a stop to reactions before they develop into conjunctivitis, if they are used early enough. Otherwise, go to the doctor for treatment.

Hepatitis is a significant health hazard in Taiwan. Type A is transmitted through food and water. When eating out, choose clean restaurants with good food and water sanitation. Use only plastic or wooden disposable chopsticks (*weisheng kwaidz*) when dining out. Reusable wooden ones cannot be adequately washed. Hepatitis B is more severe and more common, and can cause liver disease or cancer. Like AIDS it is transmitted through body fluids. Oral transmission is rare. You can protect yourself with a series of vaccinations.

Tuberculosis is a greater threat in Taiwan than in most Western countries. This disease attacks slowly, usually focusing on the lungs. It is transmitted through the sputum of infected individuals. The germs can live in dried spittle for months. This means that, again, when eating out, use only safe chopsticks and clean utensils. Use the serving spoon, rather than your own spoon, to serve from the dishes.

Sexually transmitted diseases are a cause for concern, particularly if you choose to partake to the full in any of the sexual amusements available to men on the island. Even if you have only one partner, you should be aware of the need to protect yourself and whoever you are having sex with. Although probably not as serious as in the 'play-for-pay' centers in Manila and Bangkok, possible infections run the gamut from syphilis and gonorrhea, to herpes and AIDS. There are many well-advertised clinics specializing in the treatment of foreigners with sexual diseases. They exist for a reason. Protect yourself.

Snakes, Bugs, and Mosquitoes

It has been said that, during World War II, Taiwan was a major Japanese research center in animal-based poisons, especially snakes' venom. They apparently released their stock of toxic lovelies at the end of the war. We do not know if the story is based on fact, but it is true that the island is home to cobras, vipers, coral snakes, and 'hundred-pacers' (so called because, if you are bitten by one, you die within the time it takes to walk 100 steps). For this reason, you should take precautions whenever you walk in grass, especially high grass. Make a lot of noise when walking so that snakes are startled into going about their own business, or you could use a walking stick to clear the path ahead. Carry a flashlight at night.

Beware of any snake you come across. If someone is bitten, kill the snake if possible, or at least get a complete description of its size, color, and markings. If you can, take it in a bag to the hospital so they can see what antidote to use. In the meantime, keep the victim still. You can get snake bite kits for your first aid box which show you how to extract venom, but if you don't have one you can always pack the bite in ice to slow down the spread of the poison. As soon as you can, go to the nearest emergency room, where anti-toxins are kept in stock and can be administered, providing you know which kind of snake struck. Veterans General Hospital has a special toxicology unit if you have further questions. Foreign community centers also have more information about local snakes and what the venomous ones look like.

If you live near any burial grounds, be aware that on Tomb Sweeping Day (see Chapter Eight) Taiwanese will be busy cutting down all the high grass in the tomb area. Bereft of their homes, snakes will seek new shelter, possibly behind your shoe box or under your car.

Mosquito-borne diseases like dengue fever and Japanese encephalitis are also a concern in Taiwan. It is a very good idea to put up screens in the doors and windows of your home, as well as checking on a weekly basis for any standing water that could be turning stagnant around your house. This includes flower pot trays, vases of flowers, and even toilets that are not regularly used or flushed. Repellent devices you could try are those green mosquito coils which slowly burn like incense, or their modern electric equivalent which plugs into the wall socket and releases a vapor. If you live in an area plagued by mosquitoes, you might consider getting mosquito nets for your beds, especially those of your children.

235

Hospitals

Hospitals around the world seem to be getting increasingly bureaucratic, to the detriment of health care. In the culture that invented the very concept of bureaucracy, do not expect this to be any less so. When you go to a hospital in Taiwan, take plenty of cash, your identification card (passport or alien resident certificate), and lots of patience. Be prepared to be shuttled from one desk to another, to wait, and to pay for each service in advance as it is called for by the doctor.

For instance, you have an ear infection that is driving you batty. Your spouse takes you to the hospital and you go to the reception desk. After describing your problem briefly to the clerk and requesting an English-speaking doctor, you are told you must first register and pay a registration fee. Then you will be given a queue number and a receipt that must be produced again before you go to the doctor.

After paying, you proceed to the waiting area. Show your number and receipt to the nurse in attendance. She will tell you where to wait. When your number is called, you can go in to see the doctor. He checks you over, examines your ear, asks a few questions, and gives you a prescription. When you have paid for this, show the receipt to the dispensary and you will be given your medicine.

Some hospitals now take credit cards. They will give you a small card informing the staff of each section that you are paying by credit card. They will then send the separate bills to a central desk where you can pay for them all together.

Certain hospitals also offer V.I.P. (read 'expat') services which include scheduled appointments, reduced waiting, English-speaking services, and generally less of a runaround. Expect to pay for it, though!

Clinics

An economical alternative for mild symptom ailments are the hundreds of small clinics that line the major city roads. There are also various specialty clinics (ENT stands for 'Ear, Nose, and Throat', not

'ENTerologist'). These are licenced by the health authorities and are usually run by one or two doctors-cum-entrepreneurs. They are open at convenient times, accept patients without appointments, but usually do not have English-speaking staff. You might get lucky and find a doctor who understands the vocabulary of anatomy, fever, cough, and discomfort. Otherwise, they should know what they are looking at! They will dispense a selection of pills and liquids for your problem, typically a three-day supply. The average visit will cost you about NT$500 if you book an appointment.

Pharmacies

Pharmacies in Taiwan are not controlled by the government and health authorities, the way they are in the West. Many types of medication that are only available by prescription in the West, can be bought over the counter in Taiwan, assuming you know how to ask for them in Chinese. This has its advantages and disadvantages. If you have a recurring problem, like allergies, and you know the medicine you need, you don't have to keep going to the doctor to get a supply. On the other hand, the ready availability of certain drugs, like Valium or Rogaine, means that they can just as easily be abused. Hospital dispensaries, however, will only supply drugs on the doctor's advice.

CHILD SAFETY

Your children will be in a whole new world in Taiwan. Small children, especially, are naturally outgoing and gregarious, so make sure their discoveries are safe ones.

You should make your home as childproof in Taiwan as it was in your native country, perhaps even more so. Be aware that many cleaning liquids and hazardous chemicals are produced for the local market without safety packaging and perhaps with colorful or attractive markings that young children would find new and interesting. Be sure to store all hazardous chemicals out of reach of little ones.

We have commented in Chapter Three about the traffic. In Taipei, you should never rely on drivers to stop in time not to hit you or your children. Motorized vehicles have the right of way for all practical purposes, so *do not* let your children play in the street. If they are used to riding their bikes on the road at home, take them out with you first and train them in the realities of the road in Taiwan. They should ride defensively, wear helmets, and not pull stunts.

Also, familiarize your family with the appearance of local snakes and insects. Children should be taught never to play with them.

It is a good idea to establish an 'emergency center' in your home with the names of English-speaking police, doctors, hospitals, and clinics kept close at hand. Know where the nearest hospital is and perhaps make a visit to the emergency room so you know where, what, why, and how. Remember, you are in a foreign land where the delays of language and uncertainty can mean the difference between life and death in an emergency.

Crimes against foreign children are not as prevalent in Taiwan as they are in other countries in the region, like the Philippines. Still, you should not drop your guard, especially if you have come from crime-ridden Western cities which make Taiwan seem comparatively harmless. Within school there is the same possibility that your child will fall in with a 'bad crowd', and gangs of expat children do exist, whatever you may imagine about their affluent backgrounds. You should be aware of your child's whereabouts and insist on a level of personal responsibility appropriate for their age. If you have teenage children, make sure they are aware that the laws and administration of justice in Taiwan are not the same as in their home country. The concept of *habeus corpus* and 'due process' are not the same, and the fact that they are foreigners will not protect them should they be found breaking the law.

Drugs such as marijuana, cocaine, heroin, PCP, speed, and various pills are illegal and yet still available. Penalties are stiff for possession or sale of them, but there is a growing demand. This is not to say the threat reaches anywhere near the scale of the drug problem in the West. You should be aware, though, that drugs are available and be sensitive to the signs that show your children might be trying to cope with the stress of culture shock in this way.

CRIME

Taiwan has several criminal elements. Staying clear of them is largely a matter of minding your cultural Ps and Qs and staying out of areas or situations where you are likely to stub their toes. Criminals can be roughly stratified into three groups: organized crime syndicates, disorganized youth gangs, and individuals (thieves, pickpockets, toughs, and dealers).

Organized Crime

Taiwan's organized crime groups evolved out of the secret societies of the Qing Dynasty which were patriotic organizations trying to re-establish the Ming Dynasty. They turned to crime as their cause gradually became redundant. Nowadays, they deal extensively in extortion, racketeering, prostitution, smuggling, endangered species trafficking, and live entertainment. They have also established ties with the Japanese *Yakuza* underworld. Unless you really look for trouble (like, trying to do business with them, or beating up a prostitute), you have little reason to be alarmed about them.

Gangs

Youth gangs may be of greater concern to you because their actions are driven by emotion and they are therefore less predictable. It should be noted that Taiwan protects its citizens with laws like the death penalty for armed robbery. When the rate of violent crime escalates, the officials have been known to take certain convicted felons, 'whack 'em', and (remarkably) the crime rate drops! Therefore, you are not likely to be confronted with a hood armed with more than a knife, screwdriver, or his drunken ego. That is not to say he won't be dangerous, but gentle (not groveling) persuasion, coupled with some 'face-giving' may talk you out of the mess, if, of course, you speak Mandarin! Otherwise, give them what they want, rather than 'letting them have it'.

Theft

Your house should always be properly protected, however safe you think your neighborhood is. Change the door locks once you have moved in. If you want to live in a ground floor or low level unit with access from the street, make sure it has security grills on the windows. The locals use them for a reason. Even 'controlled neighborhoods' with their own security guards still have break-ins. We recall an incident, several years ago, which occurred in a supposedly secure up-market enclave, where thieves drove a moving van up to the house, emptied it entirely of its possessions, and drove off!

There is little hope of recovering stolen items. Make an inventory of all the valuable and irreplaceable items that you own, preferably with photos, valuations, and receipts. Then get a good insurance policy.

On the Road

On the road, the chance of falling victim to crime is much higher. For example, if you have a mishap, accident, or disagreement with a taxi driver, don't be surprised if he comes after you armed with a screwdriver which he wants to plant in your intestines. Also note that citizens treat the road or area in front of their house or shop as their *own*, whether it is zoned for parking or not. The nicest of them will place a sign that says in Mandarin, "Please Do Not Park Here", while the worst will put all manner of obstacles out on the road (old chairs, cinder blocks, tires, and the like) to prevent *their* space from being taken. If you foolishly do not heed their warning, you will probably find a long, deep, rather expensive scratch or two on your car hood or door. Don't even bother reporting it to the police. Just take it to the garage workshop and call your insurance man.

If you are robbed, are in an accident where someone is injured, or your property is vandalized or stolen, call the police. Minor traffic accidents can usually be cleared up between individuals through an exchange of name cards and other details, if both parties are amicable. This information also proves you did not flee the scene of crime if the case ever ends up in court. Calling the police only involves a procedural fee that increases the cost of solving the problem.

With streets like these, parking is a nightmare in Taiwan.

FORCES OF NATURE

Two forces of nature strike Taiwan with alarming regularity: earthquakes and typhoons. The word 'typhoon' comes from the Mandarin *taifeng*. Typhoons are formed by a massive rotating weather system that is born over the Pacific, southeast of the Philippines, and they generate fast winds and heavy rains. In the Atlantic Ocean they are called hurricanes. Typhoon windspeeds can exceed 150 kilometers

241

per hour, the rain falls almost horizontally, and cars can be blown off bridges. Needless to say, public services are disrupted and water and power can be cut off for days. ICRT reports on the steady progress of typhoons approaching the island during the typhoon season in July, August, and September.

Several days before a typhoon is due to hit, make extra ice—you will need it to keep food fresh should the power go off. Keep a 'typhoon kit' in a cardboard box set aside for that purpose. You should keep in it a flashlight and spare batteries, a battery-powered radio, candles, matches, a 'sterno' or camping stove with extra cylinders of gas, some tape for taping up windows, and some empty collapsible containers to put water in. This first aid and emergency kit should be kept handy.

During the typhoon, stay inside. As the eye of the typhoon passes over, calm and clear returns, but only temporarily. The other side of the storm will hit soon. Don't be caught out in it and stay away from windows.

Taiwan is part of the Pacific Rim of Fire, the chain of volcanos and fault lines that encircle this ocean. Although it has not experienced an earthquake of the magnitude that destroyed Tangshan in China in 1976, it could happen. Tremors and earthquakes do occur here. In the event of an earthquake, get yourself and the children away from the windows and mirrors, which could shatter. Do not use the elevator when leaving a building, take the stairs. You can also crawl under a table for extra protection, or stand in a doorway.

CULTURAL QUIZ

So, you have read the book, but are you ready to try out your knowledge before subjecting the locals to your cultural *faux pas*? Just to see how much you have learned from each chapter, have a go at the true/false quiz below. Some of the answers may surprise you. Also watch out for the red herrings that have been thrown in to keep you on your toes. You may want to re-read the relevant sections referred to in the answers, depending on your score!

		True	False
1)	Taiwan is a part of China.		
2)	Because Taiwan is a tropical island, the weather is great all year round.		
3)	You can wait and get your visa at the airport when you arrive in Taiwan.		
4)	Because of the traffic problem in Taipei, it is advisable to only ride the 'wild chicken' taxis as these get you to your destination quicker.		
5)	Many expatriates in Taipei settle in the area around Tienmu or Yangmingshan.		
6)	ICRT is a local English language radio station that is very helpful to foreigners.		
7)	Real estate agents in Taiwan only get a commission from you, so they are on your side during the negotiation.		
8)	Bargaining is still an accepted practice in many stores.		
9)	A *jin* is a unit of weight.		
10)	Because Taiwan exports so many clothes to the West, fashions of all sizes are readily available.		
11)	In Taiwan, driving is a nightmare but parking is a dream.		
12)	It is easy to get along just speaking English in Taiwan.		
13)	It is possible for a foreigner to learn to speak Chinese.		
14)	Learning popular songs is a good way of improving your spoken Chinese.		
15)	A person's chop (seal) is just a relic of the past which is used for signing letters in the traditional way.		

		True	False
16)	Confucianism, Buddhism, and Taoism have had the most profound philosophical effect on the everyday life of the Taiwanese.		
17)	Because Taiwan was a colony of Japan, the Taiwanese are very similar culturally to the Japanese.		
18)	The Taiwanese have nothing but respect for foreigners, whom they see as shrewd negotiators.		
19)	Face is still very important in relating to the Taiwanese.		
20)	Chinese culture is shame-based.		
21)	*Ren ching wei* is a special, exotic, erotic, aphrodisiac dinner menu, only served on special occasions.		
22)	When giving gifts to the Taiwanese, it's the thought that counts, rather than the type, size, or brand name.		
23)	Taiwanese appreciate it if you express concern for their health and offer medical advice.		
24)	Vast sums of money are spent on weddings.		
25)	*Re nau* is the Chinese word for 'dog meat'.		
26)	Confucian etiquette demands that a check for a dinner be split between diners.		
27)	Banquet etiquette demands that you serve your partner with your chopsticks.		
28)	The Taiwanese like gambling.		
29)	*Shengyi* translates literally as 'the meaning of life' but is a general term for 'business'.		
30)	The Taiwanese prefer drawn out, relatively emotional answers to their questions, rather than a short, perfunctory 'yes' or 'no'.		

		True	False
31)	Clocks are considered good gifts because they symbolize that your friendship will last for a long time.		
32)	The importance of education to Chinese people has a history that goes back several thousand years.		
33)	If a Chinese friend has an illness, they will appreciate it if you openly express your concern for their health and tell of other people you know who had the same illness.		
34)	Confucian modesty dictates that funerals should be simple, quiet, and frugal affairs.		
35)	For a quiet night out, a fancy European-style restaurant is still the best bet in Taipei.		
36)	At the end of a restaurant meal with Taiwanese, if it is your turn to pay, it is important that you do not let them pick up the tab, regardless of who offered the dinner invitation.		
37)	During a formal Chinese banquet, it is customary to leave some of the last dish (usually rice or noodles) remaining in your bowl to signify that you have eaten your fill.		
38)	'Yellow cows' are ticket scalpers.		
39)	MTV does not mean the same thing in Taiwan that it does in the West.		
40)	The Dragon Boat Races are perhaps the only sporting event in the world inspired by a drowning bureaucrat.		
41)	During the Ghost Month, particularly cautious Taiwanese will be very careful in their undertakings and not get married or start a new business.		

		True	False
42)	In the area around Taiwan's premier university, *Tai Da*, you can find many bargains and modestly priced international restaurants.		
43)	Because Taiwanese family members work well together, your company should be encouraged to hire relatives of employees.		
44)	After eating lunch, office workers will pull their coats over their heads and take a siesta.		
45)	*Gwan syi* should be thought of as 'networking', but with Taiwanese cultural imperatives layered on.		
46)	The exchange of name cards should be done with formality to give face to the person who is presenting their card to you.		
47)	Because your Taiwanese counterpart may have invited you out for some very exotic food, you should reciprocate by taking them to a very exotic Western restaurant.		
48)	The Taiwanese drink tap water, but you should not.		
49)	Typhoons and earthquakes are potential emergencies that should be prepared for.		
50)	Because the economy is so strong and unemployment zero, there is very little crime in Taiwan.		

Answers

1) Trick question. Taiwan's political situation is exceptional. It has been a 'renegade province' of China since the Kuomintang fled the Mainland in 1949 and set up an island retreat. Read Chapter One.

2) False. Read more in Chapters One and Three.

3) False. Make sure you leave enough time to have a valid passport and visa prepared before you arrive in Taiwan.
4) False. Read more in Chapter Three.
5) True. Read more in Chapter Three.
6) True.
7) False. They get commissions from both sides. Read more in Chapter Three.
8) True and false. Fewer stores accept bargaining than in the past, but it is still acceptable in some stores and situations. Read more in Chapter Three.
9) True.
10) False.
11) False. Driving is a nightmare and you are dreaming if you think you can readily find a parking space in Taipei.
12) False. You should try to learn at least the basics to make your life in Taiwan easier. See Chapter Four.
13) True. And you should really try to do so. Read more in Chapter Four.
14) True.
15) False. The seal is a necessary article for business and identification even today. See Chapter Four.
16) True. Read more in Chapter Five.
17) True and false. Taiwan was a colony of Japan and retains close links. Many older Taiwanese can still speak Japanese, but the Taiwanese are very definitely culturally distinct from the Japanese.
18) False. Read more in Chapter Six.
19) True. Read more in Chapter Six.
20) True. Read more in Chapter Six.
21) False. Read more in Chapter Six.
22) False. Taiwanese prefer branded products that confer prestige.
23) False. Read more in Chapter Six.
24) True. Read more in Chapter Six.
25) False. Read more in Chapter Seven.
26) False. Read more in Chapter Seven.
27) False. Use the 'public use' chopsticks.
28) True.
29) True. Read more in Chapter Nine.

30) True. See Chapter Six.
31) False. See Chapter Six.
32) True. See Chapter Six.
33) False. See Chapter Six.
34) False. The opposite applies. See Chapter Six.
35) True. See Chapter Seven.
36) False. Your turn to pay comes when they accept a dinner invitation from you. If they invited you, you are expected to fight for the check but lose in the end and thank the host profusely.
37) True. See Chapter Seven.
38) True. See Chapter Eight.
39) True. It stands for 'Movie Television'. See Chapter Eight.
40) True. See Chapter Eight.
41) True. See Chapter Eight.
42) True. See Chapter Eight.
43) False. They do work well together, but with the language and other problems, you do not want a family group setting themselves up to rival you.
44) True. See Chapter Nine.
45) True. Read more about this important subject in Chapter Nine.
46) True. See Chapters Four and Nine.
47) True and false. It is perfectly proper to attempt to reciprocate, but try to be sensitive to the Taiwanese palate and help them order something they will probably enjoy. Read more in Chapter Seven.
48) False. The Taiwanese generally do not drink water straight from the tap. They boil it first. Follow this custom or get bottled water. See Chapter Ten.
49) True. See Chapter Ten.
50) False. There is less violent crime than in many Western countries but, despite its economic strength, Taiwan still has plenty of theft, gangsters, and racketeering.

BIBLIOGRAPHY

General

Taipei Bus Guide, Damien Brown. Indispensable if you will be traveling on public transport in the city.

Taipei Living, The Community Services Center, Taipei, 1991. The first book you should buy about Taiwan, after this one! It delves very deeply into areas given more cursory treatment here, such as where to buy drapes or how to get your driver's licence. It deals only briefly in cultural preparation which is the main purpose of our work. Order it, preferably before you move, from:

The Community Services Center
25, Lane 290, Chungshan North Road, Sec. 6,
Tienmu,
Taiwan
Tel: 886-2-8368134   Fax: 886-2-8352530

Contact this organization when you arrive as well. They can be very helpful.

The Times Travel Library: Taipei, Paul Mooney. Times Editions, Singapore, 1988. A picture book with surprisingly good insights into things to do and see in Taipei.

Insight Guides: *Taiwan*, Daniel Reid. APA Publications, Hong Kong, 1989. An excellent guide book to the island's many nooks and crannies, with a good many cultural insights. Written by a fellow long-term Taiwan resident and student of Chris's late martial arts master.

This Month in Taiwan.
Not a book, but a magazine and free at that! This indispensable

250

magazine can be picked up at any good hotel. It has useful addresses and phone numbers, basic maps, hotel and restaurant lists, advertisements for many services you might need, and the latest news about the doings in the expatriate community.

Doing Business
Doing Business in the Republic of China, James Cheng. Cheng and Cheng Law Offices, Taipei, 1982. Some party-line history and lots of legal boiler plate, but invaluable if you intend to set up a company in Taiwan.

History
The Soong Dynasy, Sterling Seagraves. Sidgewick and Jackson, London, 1985. This author certainly took off the gloves when he wrote about the three Soong sisters, whose powerful family origins and highly political marriages partly shaped modern China. It also reveals a darker side to the history of the Kuomintang in Mainland China.

Formosa Betrayed, George Kerr. Houghton Mifflin, Boston, 1965. A detailed account of U.S. involvement in Taiwan after World War II, along with a frank description of the infamous *Er Er Ba* Massacre. You will not find it in Taiwan. Look in your college library at home.

Taoism, Buddhism, and Confucianism
The Tao of Health, Sex, and Longevity: A Modern Practical Guide to the Ancient Way and ***Guarding the Three Treasures***, Daniel Reid.
Both these highly readable books deal with the practical application of Taoist medical theory in building your own longevity program.

Also look out for books by Thomas Cleary, a prolific and lucid translator who has focused on ancient masterpieces of Chinese and

251

Japanese thought. R. L. Wing has also done some good practical translations of Taoist thought.

An Alternative View
The Ugly Chinaman and the Crisis of Chinese Culture, Bo Yang, translated and edited by J. Cohn and Jing Qing. Allen and Unwin, St. Leonards, New South Wales, 1992. A former political prisoner in Taiwan, Bo Yang minutely details the negative sides of the Chinese persona.

If you cannot get these titles in your country, you can find most of them at:

Caves Bookstore,
103 Chungshan North Road, Sec. 2,
Taipei,
Taiwan

This shop has long been a first stop for people visiting Taiwan.

THE AUTHORS

Wu Ling-li was born and bred in an old and traditional part of downtown Taipei. She grew up in an extended family of grandparents, parents, aunts and uncles, and then tested her way up the academic ladder to win herself a place at Providence College, where she studied Business Science.

Chris Bates was bounced around between Atlanta, Georgia, and Fairfield, Connecticut for the first 17 years of his life, until he pursued a lifelong dream of training in Asian martial arts. He took a Bachelor of Arts degree in Chinese Studies and spent his senior year at Tunghai University in Taichung, Taiwan.

Through *yuan fen* (the principle that the fates of two people are inextricably entwined), Chris and Ling-li met whilst at college in Taichung in 1977. They were married a year later. Their life together has taken them on several tours of the United States (one year each), one tour of Taiwan (six years), and two tours of Singapore (eight years in total). They have worked for Western companies and have certainly endured their share of culture shock.

Much of their time, they believe, has been spent at the interface of the expatriate and local communities. Ling-li has befriended many Westerners in her climb to a Masters ranking in American contract bridge, while Chris has befriended many Taiwanese, training in Burmese and Chinese martial arts under some of the finest masters alive.

Chris and Ling-li presently manage their own business, providing market research and management consulting services to both Western and Asian companies. They have three children.

Chris is the author of *The Wave Man* (Times Editions, Singapore, 1993), a thriller set in Asia and acclaimed for its authenticity. *Culture Shock! Taiwan* is their first collaborative work.

INDEX

A

Accommodation 31-33, 37-38
Addresses 64-65
Air travel 25-26
Alien resident certificate 28

B

Banquets 175-179
Bargaining 44-47
Bathrooms 154-156
Bicycles 63
Body language 85-87, 124-125
Buddhism 98-100
Buses 31, 62-63

C

Cars 57-60
Chiang Kai Shek 18-22, 191, 195
Children 135-138, 237- 239
Chinese New Year 187-190
Chop (seal) 92-93, 213
Cinema 181-183, 189
Clothes 52-55, 215-216
Clubs 65, 71
Confucianism 95-98, 150
Corruption 222
Crime 239-241
Customs and immigration 29-30

D

Dining out 160-161, 170-175,
    213-214, 223-225·
Domestic help 41-43

E

Engagements 140-141

F

'Face' 43, 125-130, 141, 171,
    175, 211, 216, 219, 224-225
Family 97-98, 126-127, 134-136,
    150-151, 159-160, 208-210
Feng shwei 107-108, 149
Festivals 187-195
Food 229-232
    groceries 47-52
    breakfast 159-160
    lunch 160
    dinner 160-161
Funerals 145-150

G

Gambling 184-185, 189
Geography 11-13
Ghosts 110-114
    ghost month 193-194
Gifts 131-133, 138, 142-144,
    148, 188, 218-219
Gwan syi 214-219

H

Hakka 14, 162
Health 144, 228, 233-234, 236-
    237
Hospitals 236
Hostesses 225

J

Japan, influence of 16-18, 165, 169, 205
Jin (unit of weight) 51-52

K

Karaoke 183-184, 223
Kuomintang 18-21

L

Libraries 66
Lunar calendar 109-110

M

Markets 48-52
Martial arts 108-109
Mass Rapid Transit 63
Medicine 104-106, 231-232, 237
Motorcycles 60-62
MTV 183

N

Names 89-92, 119-120
name cards 90-91, 216

O

Opera 186

P

Parking 57-58, 240
Phonetic symbols 77-78
Pollution 33, 232-233

R

Re nau 158, 181
Relationships 150-153
Ren ching wei 130-131, 164, 171, 221-222

S

Schools 67
Shame 126, 138
Shopping 43-54
Smoking 233
Snakes 166-167, 234-235
Spirit worship 110-112, 114, 117, 193-194
temples 113-117

T

Table manners 173-174
Tai Du (Taiwan Independence) 20, 22, 95
Taoism 100-104
Taxis 30-31, 56
Tea-drinking 169-170

Traffic 55-56
Transport 55-63
Trekking 200-201
Typhoons 13, 241-242

V

Visas 26-29
Voltage 40-41

W

Wai Sheng Ren 20, 159, 161
Walking 63
Weather 13, 52-53, 55
Weddings 141-142
Welcoming services 65-66
Work permits 27-28

Y

Yuan fen 140

Z

Zodiac (Chinese) 110